T0246900

Say Yes

FOUNDATIONAL LESSONS
from Combat Town, the Quigley,
and Taking Invisible Paths

JON MICHAELS

SAY YES

Foundational Lessons from Combat Town, the Quigley, and Taking Invisible Paths

© 2024, Jon Michaels

ISBN: 979-8-35097-961-9 (soft cover)
ISBN: 979-8-35096-643-5 (hard cover)
ISBN: 979-8-35097-641-0 (eBook)

To our boys, Wheeler and Tavis.

Your Mom and I are proud of all you have accomplished

and look forward to seeing what new challenges

and opportunities you seize next.

CONTENTS

INTRODUCTION

"DID YOU HEAR ABOUT THE SPEECH THE Navy SEAL gave?"

That question was posed to me back in the late spring of 2014. Having spent just shy of ten years in the Marines, more than fifteen months deployed aboard Navy ships around the world, and having interacted with a few SEALs along the way, I can tell you that the first thing that comes to mind when thinking about Navy SEALs is *not* their prowess at giving speeches.

"No, but maybe I should check it out."

In this particular instance, Navy Admiral William McRaven had given the 2014 commencement address at the University of Texas at Austin graduation. The ten-minute video of the speech quickly went viral. Admiral McRaven spent more than thirty-seven years in uniform, most notably in his final role as the head of the United States Special Operations Command, and is credited with organizing and overseeing the execution of Operation Neptune Spear, the special ops raid that led to the killing of Osama bin Laden in May 2011. McRaven has seen a thing or two, that's for sure.

He expanded that commencement address into the 2017 book *Make Your Bed: Little Things That Can Change Your Life . . . And Maybe the World.* It is a collection of short stories and lessons from his military training and how those lessons translate into advice that can profoundly influence the lives of others. That short book contains a masterclass in leadership and discipline.

Fast forward to 2023, when Navy Captain Brett Crozier penned *Surf When You Can: Lessons in Life, Loyalty, and Leadership from a Maverick Navy Captain.* I was intrigued by the story of an officer who spent thirty years in the Navy and a decade working to become the commanding officer of the aircraft carrier USS *Theodore Roosevelt*, perhaps the mightiest weapon in the United States arsenal, and then was relieved of that command after only a few months due to controversy over his proactive handling of COVID-19. *What can one learn from such a person and their experiences?*

His memoir has some similarities to Admiral McRaven's in that they both draw on foundational experiences as junior officers and how those events helped shape their approach to leadership in their ensuing decades of service.

Those two books led me to think about my own experiences as a junior officer in the military and the moments that helped me develop insights and led to me taking distinct actions later in my career. It was those experiences and lessons from the military that shaped who I am and how I operate. At the same time, my athletic endeavors (while admittedly at a recreational level) have been important for me as well, much as Captain Crozier speaks about the importance of surfing as part of his lifestyle.

Let's pause for a moment and recognize that in mentioning these two distinguished officers I am in no way attempting to compare my military career to those of Admiral McRaven and Captain Crozier. I was an active duty Marine for just shy of ten years and had the privilege to serve as an officer and naval aviator. Theirs were much longer careers with a different level of service, accomplishment, and significance. There is no doubt about it.

We do have something in common, though: All three of us were at one point junior officers in the military. We all completed initial officer training and took away lifelong lessons from that period. We all led small units in the early part of our career and learned invaluable lessons from those opportunities. We each took the time to reflect on how those early, poignant events helped shape our character in later years. With that, I want to recognize Admiral McRaven and Captain Crozier for the inspiration to capture in words my early career experiences and how they have shaped my actions in the ensuing decades.

As a parent, I am always thinking about how to develop my two boys physically, mentally, and emotionally. The lessons from Admiral McRaven and Captain Crozier led me to think about the early events in my professional life and the meaning they held for me. *Maybe there are lessons there my boys could learn from,* I thought, so I put pen to paper with the specific intention of capturing these stories and lessons for them.

This book is about the key moments that happen to each and every one of us in the course of our lives. If we seize and learn from those moments, they can have profound impacts on our personal and professional development in the years and decades that follow. The problem is, these are often seemingly small or inconsequential events at the time, and we default to missing out on the growth opportunities they could bring. A person is fortunate if they can recognize that even one of these foundational events has occurred and is able to learn from it.

For me, the military and athletics provided many of those events. The day I got my butt chewed by a two-star general. The day I said "No" to a prestigious military training program. The day I flew a shoebox containing a single helicopter part halfway across California and started thinking differently about how we use energy. The day I took a wrong turn on a trail run and how that led to me asking better questions at work. The day I swam from Alcatraz in a race and gained a new appreciation for learning new skills. So, while many of these stories center on an experience from the military, this isn't a book about the military. This book is about encouraging everyone to seek out those moments in their own lives and grasp the lessons they offer.

I freely admit that the themes I write about were inspired by Admiral McRaven and Captain Crozier. In fact, a close observer will notice that Admiral McRaven writes about "Build the best damn frog float you can" in his 2023 book *The Wisdom of the Bullfrog: Leadership Made Simple (But Not Easy)*. That inspired me to write about my personal experience with "Run the best damn geedunk you can" in chapter eight. Any similarities you see are likely in part because most junior officers experience comparable situations early in their careers. One difference, however, is what lessons are gleaned from those events and how they manifest themselves in the individual (and those they interact with) years and decades later.

Personal and professional development is a path. It's not always a straight line, and you don't always know where it's going to lead. Here are stories from my path, and I trust there are some nuggets that will be thought-provoking for you as you uncover your own foundational stories that can help you become the best version of yourself.

CHAPTER ONE

Little Things Matter More than You Think

If you want to be the best version of yourself,
know that the way you do little things
is the way you do everything.

MARINE OFFICER CANDIDATE SCHOOL (OCS) is a ten-week test of perseverance. Most candidates, like me, enter the barracks at Quantico as recent college graduates who are seeking a challenge, want to make a difference, and see becoming a leader of Marines as their way of pursuing that challenge. OCS is the Marine Corps' way of figuring out if you have what it takes.

There are multiple ways to become a Marine officer. Perhaps the most well-known is to graduate from the Naval Academy in Annapolis, Maryland. Another is to complete Naval Reserve Officers Training Corps (ROTC) while attending a participating college or university.

A third path is the one I chose, which runs through Quantico, Virginia, and involves attending OCS.

OCS is located among the pine trees and rolling hills of Marine Corps Base Quantico, about thirty miles southwest of Washington, DC, along the west shore of the Potomac River. Known as the Crossroads of the Corps, Quantico is home to multiple Marine units that include the Marine Corps Combat Development Command and Marine Corps Air Station Quantico, home to HMX-1. If that last alpha-numeric combination doesn't ring a bell, perhaps you have seen those iconic green-and-white-topped helicopters that fly the president around; HMX-1 is the name of that squadron. The base is also home to the FBI Academy, FBI Laboratory, and Drug Enforcement Agency Training Academy, among others. Quantico is a large base, and OCS takes up a very small part of it.

The facilities of OCS are simple yet functional—barracks for sleeping, a large parade ground for marching and close-order drill, grass fields for physical training, and the surrounding terrain of gravel trails and dense woods for land-navigation exercises. It is these basic facilities where officer candidates are trained and evaluated on their leadership skills, academics, and physical fitness. The leadership evaluations are based on command presence, communication skills, decision-making, and the ability to lead subordinates. I remember feeling excited, nervous, and more than a little bit scared in taking that first step off the bus and onto those grounds.

The military is a world unfamiliar to most. It starts with two days of administrative intake that encompasses getting haircuts, procuring uniforms, and completing medical screenings. Basic onboarding activities needed to be completed, and it wasn't until the end of those first two days that we met our commanding officer, the colonel who led OCS.

The colonel gave a short talk that morning. He not only commanded the unit but our attention as well. He didn't have to say much to have an impact on each of us when he introduced us to fierce historical battles like Iwo Jima and Belleau Wood and exposed us to names of legendary Marine warriors like Chesty Puller and Smedley Butler. As he brought his comments that afternoon to a close, he finished with, "Platoon commanders, carry out the plan of the day," and then smartly about-faced and left the room.

The platoon commanders then stepped to the center of the room, and the senior one commanded, "Platoon sergeants, carry out the plan of the day." Those captains about-faced and walked down the long center aisle and out the back of the hall.

Then it was quiet. For about three seconds. The next ten weeks would be like nothing I had ever experienced before. It changed my life in those moments and for many decades following.

Though common in movies and TV, the title "Drill Instructor" isn't used at OCS. The enlisted staff sergeants are rather referred to as a platoon sergeant or sergeant instructor, the former being the senior of the two. I'll just refer to them collectively as platoon sergeant here, as it's not important to distinguish between the two for what I'm sharing.

Titles didn't matter anyway at this point. The collective group descended on the candidates and started doing what they do best: Making Marine officers. It was a blur of shouted commands, sounding off, and starting to live in this new world. In the next few days we learned to march, tackled the obstacle course, and battled with pugil sticks (picture a broomstick with large, heavy padding on each end, kind of like a giant cotton swab, that is used to simulate close-quarters combat with a rifle and bayonet). Some of the most important and memorable lessons, though, were the ones that weren't formally on the training schedule. Instead, these seemingly impromptu lessons (but likely planned as they are good at what they do) taught by those platoon sergeants helped us understand that the way you do little things is the way you will likely do big things.

My first lesson in understanding the importance of these little things came two days after the colonel's welcome. Our platoon sergeants had been giving us a crash course in all things military that included how to properly wear the uniform, how to polish our boots, and how to salute smartly. One of the biggest and most visible was how to march as a unified group. We've all seen it in the movies as the salty sergeant calls out, "Left, right, left, right," and the perfectly aligned rows and columns of Marines march in impressive unison. Simple, right? That's what I thought, too, until I found out I was chosen as the first candidate to spend two days serving as the candidate platoon sergeant. Talk about learning a hard lesson about the importance of little things.

Officer candidates are assigned turns acting in different leadership roles; one small way of learning and being evaluated, at the same time. As the candidate platoon sergeant, I took on the responsibilities of the actual platoon sergeant; no small feat considering he had more than a dozen years of military experience and I had a whopping two days.

My first task that day was to march our platoon to the chow hall for breakfast. I stood before the assembled platoon and called, "Right face. Forward march." Off we went. The first few steps were smooth, and I started to consider myself a quick learner.

They are doing it? This is great!

It was great until we made it to a small footbridge that would take us the final steps to the chow hall. I needed our platoon to make a right turn and was attempting to calculate when exactly to give the "Column right, march" command. At the perfect moment I gave the command... and then all hell broke loose.

I should share at this point a finer point about giving commands to a marching platoon. There are various commands you can give: column right, column half-right, mark time, and halt, to name a few. These commands are given in rapid fire components broken down into syllables that sound like "Col-umn right, march" with each syllable perfectly aligning with a left or right foot strike. The key to having the platoon move in perfect unison is to begin the first syllable of the command, "col" in this situation, on the proper left or right foot strike. With all of a few days of military training behind me, that was a nuance I had yet to master. So in addition to initiating my command on the wrong foot strike, I was also a bit nervous and commanded the platoon to turn left instead of right.

Half the platoon started to turn left as I commanded them to do. The other half, obviously knowing a right turn was the proper way to take us to the chow hall, pivoted that way. Combine that with my mistake of initiating the command on the wrong foot, and it took less than a second for the entire platoon to be facing four different directions and scattered like kids on a playground.

"Candidate Michaels! What is going on? What are you doing?" The platoon sergeant's language may have been a bit more colorful than that.

I didn't have an answer as I looked at the other candidates and they looked at me. The stare of the platoon sergeant said all that needed to be said. I hadn't listened and paid attention enough to fully grasp the importance of how you command a group while marching. It's so simple . . . if you understand the basics. If you can't march a platoon, how can you lead them in combat?

That was my first lesson in understanding the importance of little things and doing them properly.

We soon took our initial Physical Fitness Test (PFT), and that proved to be yet another lesson.

The PFT is one of the first activities at OCS. At the time, the PFT consisted of three parts: a three-mile run, pull-ups, and sit-ups. To get the maximum score, you needed to run the three miles in eighteen minutes or less, perform twenty pull-ups, and then one hundred sit-ups. One area of your performance at OCS you can control is how well conditioned you are when you arrive; my previous best was just under nineteen minutes for the three miles. My adrenaline was pumping that morning of the initial PFT. I ran an 18:09 . . . a personal best! The smile on my face lasted but a few seconds until our platoon sergeant got in my face and let it fly.

"Candidate Michaels! What was that? I guess you decided to just not try today and give up at the end, huh? (again, his words were slightly more colorful). And you want to be an officer in my Marine Corps?" He berated my obvious lackluster effort (to him, at least) for a bit longer before finishing with a curt, "Get out of here!"

Still breathing hard, I smartly about-faced and got out of there as fast as I could. Eighteen minutes and nine seconds. It was a good run, a great run in my mind, but I came up a bit short at the end. Nine seconds short. About how long it takes to tie your shoes. Doesn't matter that it was a personal best; it still could've been just a little bit better, and the platoon sergeant didn't let it pass. He was concerned that the way I did that little thing was the way I would respond to the bigger challenges to come.

In the Marines, it's not just about you. Everyone's always watching. Your team and the entire organization see every move you make. And the Marines under an officer's command will be deciding if they think you have what it takes.

The Leadership Reaction Course is a group of challenges and obstacles carried out as a four-man fire team, where every candidate must take the role of team leader and receive a mission, develop a plan, issue their orders, and then execute.

As our platoon commander finished his instructions for the exercise, one of the candidates asked, "Sir, are we being timed on this? Are we on the clock?"

There wasn't a second's hesitation in his reply. "As a Marine officer, you are always being timed. You are always on the clock. The Marines in your command will watch and evaluate everything you do. How you dress. How you stand. How you walk. How you run. How you speak."

His final comment was the one that left an impression on all of us.

"Your Marines are always watching." The unspoken meaning was that every action we took—large and small—would be constantly evaluated by the Marines under our command. I took that lesson to heart and have applied it to how I do everything decades later—from family interactions to my corporate career.

The Quigley was another example the platoon sergeants used to impress upon us how much little things count and how they were crucial parts of the larger things we did.

A daunting event at OCS is the Combat Course, a combination of a forced march, endurance course, and mud run, culminated by swimming through the muddy, snake-infested waters of the Quigley. Devised by First Lieutenant William Quigley in 1967, the Quigley greets officer candidates with foul-smelling water, barbed wire, submerged concrete culverts and logs, and continues for about fifty yards. A civilian would likely take a quick look at it and promptly turn around, while Marines officers smirk when they think of it and remember having to navigate the nastiness of the Quigley while in full combat gear and carrying an M16A2 rifle in order to complete the Combat Course.

The Combat Course is a timed and graded event that weighs heavily on your overall ranking for graduation. You can run, jump, and climb faster than anyone on the course, but there is a final check as you navigate the Quigley and cross the finish line. Your platoon sergeant examines your rifle and checks to see if the muzzle is clear. You can have the fastest time across the finish line, but if your muzzle isn't clean and a round would have been obstructed on the way out of your weapon, well, that just means disqualification for that event.

I saw this with one candidate who didn't finish OCS and was sent home in week seven. He was almost done! This particular candidate had struggled for a while and was having trouble making the grade. He struggled with uniform inspections and maintaining his bearing when in a leadership position within the platoon.

I think his final undoing was the Combat Course and the Quigley. This particular candidate was in good physical condition, but on the day, that one moment of inattention and just a small amount of dirt inside his muzzle made all his previous efforts worthless. A little dirt may not seem like much, and that one single thing likely wasn't the only thing sent him home. But after weeks of missteps and trouble, the idea that his rifle would misfire at the moment he, and his Marines, were counting on it was too much to bear. A failing grade there, and he was on his way home.

At this point you may be thinking, *Sure, little things are important in the military, and the same is true of professional sports and some other professions like being a doctor. But I'm not going to be one of those, so does this really matter to me?*

Yes.

Consider this . . . perhaps you are a baker. It doesn't take a lot of yeast to make bread, but without it you really don't have bread. Maybe you are an architect or structural engineer designing an office tower or bridge. Think attention to detail doesn't matter there? If you were falsely accused of a crime and on trial, you surely would want your lawyer to focus on every little detail of the case.

I'm hard pressed to think of any profession, career, hobby, anything, where little details don't matter a lot.

My ten years in the Marines was memorable in real time, but it also has affected how I view the world now that I've transitioned to a civilian career. Perhaps one of the lessons I tap into most is this idea about how much the little things we do have a huge impact on the big picture. In fact, I applied it to remedy a persistent problem that existed when I joined the team at Volta. I used it to overcome the Operations team's tendency to focus their strategies around two terms I sought to abolish: hope and wait.

Volta built electric vehicle charging stations at locations like shopping malls and grocery stores. I joined in the fall of 2016 when it was a scrappy, twenty-five-person startup with a small number of installed charging stations but grand plans to grow and expand across the United States and abroad.

Anyone who knows me knows I loathe the idea of hoping and waiting for anything to happen. It leaves too much to doubt and often raises unrealistic hopes of something that might happen if someone else were to take action.

There was a day as the head of Operations at Volta when one of our construction project managers was briefing me on the status of a particularly important project.

He finished, "So then I told the client that we are waiting for our external engineering partner to follow up on getting the permits in place and that I hope we can get the stations installed in the next few weeks."

I was flabbergasted. *What did he tell our customer? He's waiting for another entity, that the client probably doesn't even know exists, to complete one of the most crucial tasks in the overall project timeline? He's responsible for that crucial task and has no idea when it will be complete?*

I want to give my teams the leeway to run projects the way they see fit, but this was going too far. You don't build trust by saying things that make it sound like you're not in control of projects others have delegated to you to manage. Worse is being in the dark about what's actually happening. Hoping doesn't propel a small startup into places and spaces that foster rapid growth.

At our next team meeting, I set a new expectation and standing rule. We were not allowed to speak, let alone think, the words *hoping* or *waiting*. They were to be immediately banished from our vocabulary. "No one on this team will hope or wait for anything. That's not a technique professionals use, and it's not going to be part of how we operate," was my guidance.

The faces in the room were quiet at first. After a slight pause there were some head nods, and it seemed they heard my message and intent.

Not five minutes later, a project manager, and a different one this time, reported, "I'm hoping to have this project complete by the end of the month."

I could see we had a bigger issue at hand and were going to have to take a different approach. With a degree in psychology, I try to consider unique ways to explore social dynamics and decided to gamify this situation. At our next team meeting, I introduced the Dollar Jar and explained how it worked.

"This jar is your new friend. This jar is going to help us all. This jar is going to remind you, with every word you speak and intention you think, that hoping and waiting are not only words we are not going to say on this team, they are concepts we are not even going to think."

This jar was not some mystical chalice or ornate device but rather a simple pint glass with a piece of paper taped on it that had the word "Hoping" written in black ink on one side and the word "Waiting" written on the other. Both were surrounded with a bright red circle with a red diagonal line passing right through the middle of the words.

The rules were simple. "Every time any of us says 'hoping' or 'waiting,' the speaker is going to put a dollar in the jar. We are going to be relentless about this, starting right now. More importantly, this is not just about these two words. It's about the actions we are going to take instead of using these two words. We are going to develop timeframes and plans. We are going to follow-up. We are going to pick up the phone and make calls. We are going to do lots of things, and we are not going to hope or wait."

I collected three dollars in the jar before the end of that first meeting.

In the ensuing weeks, many project managers thought it was silly when I stopped them at the end of a sentence and asked, "What did you say?" They would pause, then I could see them rewind the prior sentence in their head, realizing they had uttered one of the banned words. More dollars in the jar.

A subtle shift started to happen after a few weeks. I knew the concept I wanted the team to embrace was starting to take hold. A sentence would start with, "After we get the construction drawings signed off by the client, we can submit for the permits and I ho—" Then silence. Their eyes would dart left to right, pause momentarily, then dart back to left. They had started to say the word but caught themselves. Another brief pause, followed by, "After we get the construction drawings signed off by the client, I am going to follow up directly with the engineering firm to ensure the permit package is submitted the next day and we get an expected permitting date from the jurisdiction."

Whoa. We are onto something.

Instances like that increased in the coming weeks and months. We still saw some dollars deposited into the jar—mindsets don't change overnight—but they did eventually slow. You can never completely change something like this, and I have to admit I had to put a few dollars into the jar myself.

This mindset did more than impact just our Operations team: It started to spread throughout the organization. One of our project managers heard a member of the Finance team speak about how they were hoping to finish the quarterly close on time and called out the use of the word. Heck, I even called out our CEO when he hoped something would happen on time. Another dollar in the jar.

The platoon sergeants at OCS worked hard to have us understand that the way you do little things is the way you do everything. How you march, how you clean your rifle, the effort you put into everyday actions. Those concepts carry into the civilian world.

I kept that jar on my desk, and every time I saw it I thought of OCS and marching on the parade deck. I was reminded of how easy it is to get the whole team going in different, wrong directions by failing to notice the little things.

A single word is more than just a word. A dollar is more than a dollar. Little things matter. If you want to be the best version of yourself, know that the way you do little things is the way you do everything.

CHAPTER TWO

Seize Unexpected Opportunities

If you want to be the best version of yourself,
look for the invisible path,
as that is where the adventure begins.

MANY PEOPLE SUFFER FROM THE MISCON-
ception that professional careers should follow a path. Start here, do this next, spend time doing that, and you are sure to be on the track to success. It starts early in our schooling with second grade, third grade, fourth grade and continues all the way through sophomore, junior, senior, and beyond. We are trained that there is a predetermined progression, and that's just not true of professional careers. I've found that it's not that there is no path, or that you shouldn't follow one, but rather that there may be a path before you and it's not the one you envisioned. Sometimes you don't consider an opportunity because you aren't sure where the ensuing path will lead. I've heard this referred to as an *invisible path*. It's one I've taken to seize unexpected opportunities at multiple points in my career.

I entered the University of Pennsylvania as an engineering student. Convinced this was a great path for me because I did very well in high school physics and calculus, I figured my future was set. After two years of college, I realized an engineering career would make me miserable. So, in my junior year, I switched my major to psychology. The problem was, even though I enjoyed the social and organizational behavior aspects of psychology, and still benefit from those learning opportunities today, not many companies are screaming for psychology majors to fill critical roles. Friends in my social circles were going to law school, medical school, or Wall Street. None of those appealed to me, which left me with no concrete plans after graduation. That clear path I had chosen disappeared once I stepped away from my math and science roots. It was toward the end of my junior year in college when a glimpse of that first invisible path showed up.

While home on a break toward the end of that spring semester, I received a postcard in the mail from the Marines, informing me of all the great Montgomery GI Bill benefits I could earn by enlisting in the Corps. I wasn't about to drop out of Penn and enlist, but that postcard planted a seed and got me thinking.

My post-graduation future gnawed at me for a while. *I want to do something meaningful. I want to do something bigger than myself. I want to do something cool.* That postcard: *The Few. The Proud. The Marines.*

There was a Marine recruiting office in downtown Philadelphia. I struck up the courage to walk in. It wasn't much of an office—some spartan desks and a few metal chairs—but the posters on the walls spoke to me. There were Marines rappelling down towers, driving tanks, advancing on a beach in an inflatable boat, faces camouflaged and looking like the kind of people you didn't want to mess with. *I think I'm in the right place.* I couldn't tell you which of those things I wanted to do, but I could tell you I wanted to be a Marine.

I'm sure the staff sergeant looked at me a bit questioningly as I walked in, and I suspect his thinking changed with my opening words when I proudly declared, "I want to join the Marines. How do I sign up?"

I can only imagine his next thought, *Excellent. I've got an easy one here.*

We sat down and talked about the Marines and what it was like to wear the uniform. The staff sergeant I was speaking with, and the captain who soon joined us, were every bit the warriors and professionals I had envisioned. They told me about OCS, the ten-week program where recent college graduates would be trained and molded into officers, and then The Basic School (TBS), where every officer, regardless of their future role in the Corps, had to first learn how to be an infantry platoon commander. This was what I wanted.

"So, is it hard to get accepted into OCS? What are my chances of getting in?"

The captain shared with me the many different options that could await me after finishing OCS and TBS training. Some, like infantry, intelligence, and combat engineering, sounded like what I might be looking for, but my ears really perked up when he calmly stated, "Well, we are also looking for pilots right now, so if you put in a flight application, you should have a pretty good shot."

Wait. What? Be a pilot? Really?

There is an SAT-like test as part of applying to flight school. I suspect the captain figured that if I was smart enough to get myself into Penn, I was probably smart enough to score well on another standardized, multiple-choice test. As it turned out, I was.

The funny thing is that if you ask military pilots about their flying ambitions, many will say something along the lines of, "Ever since I was four years old . . . all I've wanted to do was fly a plane." In my case, I was twenty years old, and a person I'd known for fifteen minutes said to me, "Do you want to fly?" My response after a short pause was, "Okay."

After graduation I was off to Officer Candidate School, The Basic School, and then Flight School. I did well there and was assigned my first choice of aircraft, the CH-53E Super Stallion. I was well on my way to a career in the Marines and could have pursued that route. Then an event in the fall of 2000 changed my thinking. Another invisible path appeared that would have a big impact on the decisions I later made in my corporate career.

I was assigned to another squadron, the Purple Foxes of Marine Medium Helicopter Squadron 268 (Reinforced), and the 11th Marine Expeditionary Unit (Special Operations Capable) in the fall of 2000. We were starting our six-month workups where Marine ground and air forces came together to practice more than twenty different missions we would need to be able to perform in as little as six hours from receipt of the mission to commencing execution. The squadron was a mix of four types of helicopters that included CH-53E Super Stallions, CH-46E Sea Knights, AH-1W Cobras, and UH-1N Hueys, as well as AV-8B Harrier jets. On this day, different aircraft types were performing missions, and we had a detachment of CH-46s operating out of an airfield in the San Francisco Bay Area of Northern California.

One of the CH-46s needed a replacement actuator, quite a simple thing to procure and fix. Actuators are metal tubes that are part of the mechanical flight control system; they translate pilot movements from the cockpit to the systems that control how the helicopter moves. This specific piece was about the size of your forearm and easily would have fit inside a typical shoebox. FedEx could have delivered it overnight for less than $50, and the flightline crew could have made the switch and completed the repair the next day.

The military is a unique beast, though, and chose not to take that seemingly simple course of action. As we were getting closer to the end of the fiscal year, our operations officer (OpsO) reminded us that we had an allotment of flight hours that needed to be used before the end of the month; if you don't use your full allotment in a given year, you can expect to receive a smaller allotment the following year.

That became my lucky day, as we had more hours to fly in a shortening period before the end of the month (and fiscal year). The OpsO decided to have us fly the needed actuator up to Northern California from our base down in San Diego.

Pilots like to think about flying in sections, or pairs, and with the need to fly more hours, the OpsO also decided to send a section of CH-53s on the flight. It was a glorious day to be the section leader; the California coastline is beautiful. The crew of both aircraft enjoyed every minute of the three-hour flight up and three-hour flight back.

Do some quick math on two aircraft at six flight hours each to the tune of roughly $13,000 per flight hour (at the time) and then compare that to what could have been a $50 overnight shipping expense.

Sure, it was fun, and I was happy to get the flight time on a beautiful day, but heading home that evening I couldn't help but think about how wasteful it was. It was aviation fuel in that instance and made me think about energy more generally and how we need to be more mindful of how we use it.

That one day and six flight hours stayed with me for years, tucked away in the back of my mind like when you dogear a page in a book and are not quite sure why; you know there is a nugget on that page you think you'll want to come back to but aren't sure how it's going to apply to your future life. I would think about that box and single part and all the wasted resources that went into getting it to its destination. I didn't know it at the time, but that little box would stay with me for the better part of a decade to become a big part of my future decisions—another one of those invisible paths.

I thought about that box during graduate school, where I pursued a master's degree in business. I continued to think about that box after graduating and joining my family's jewelry business that my great-great-grandfather had started way back in 1885. I learned a great deal about retail operations and customer service from that experience but realized that while retail jewelry was in my blood, it was not my passion. Selling rings and necklaces wasn't getting me fired up when I woke up in the morning. It was time to change my path. That day, back in the fall of 2000, and that box and that part had been on my mind ever since we had spent $78,000 to go get it. It was time to do something about it.

My next path was to join a Boston-based tech company, EnerNOC, that was helping commercial and industrial businesses make better decisions about how to buy energy, when to use it, and how much to use. I joined in the fall of 2008 as an individual contributor project manager, working from their San Francisco office. I had nearly ten years as a Marine, a graduate degree in business, and then two additional years of work experience. I felt I was ready for more than an individual contributor role but spent that next year working as hard as I could to learn a new business from the ground up. A year later I was promoted into a management position that had me leading the Field Operations team in the western part of the US.

As I was wondering what might be in store for me beyond Operations, a different path opened up for me a few years later. EnerNOC was bringing a new enterprise software as a service (SaaS) platform to the market to help organizations better manage their energy use. The company needed a sales team capable of selling a technical product to a wide variety of large organizations. The existing sales team would be complemented by a new sales engineering team. I was asked to lead that new team and develop that new function. I was the first sales engineer. Soon after, we had a start-up team of five. Two years after standing up, we had a team of twenty sales engineers across North America, Europe, and Australia. An interesting point about this path was that the term "sales engineer" was one I hadn't even heard of until we got into the details of forming this team.

After several years, and multiple roles at that company, another invisible path reared its head when a former coworker called to tell me about this cool Bay Area startup she was at that was getting ready for a new stage of growth. That was Volta, and I would never have guessed at that time the different paths that would ultimately open up to me. Taking that phone call opened an entirely new path.

I started leading the Operations team at Volta and was responsible for supply chain, project design, and construction, as well as ongoing operations and maintenance. After four years and leading the installation of more than fifteen hundred EV charging stations and expanding to fifteen new states across the country, I was asked to lead a new Network Development team that included our sales, network planning, and enterprise account management teams. I had never led a sales organization before, and the network planning team needed to be built from scratch. That unexpected experience was foundational for me in building my ability to lead diverse teams.

As we grew, an ongoing challenge for the San Francisco-based Volta was that we often fell into the trap of having a California-centric view of things. That was not how we were going to be successful in Chicago, Dallas, Boston, Los Angeles, and other cities across America. To combat that challenge, I led the development of a new regional general manager (GM) function. These GMs were to be our business leaders and brand ambassadors as we grew our operations in cities across the country. Building and leading new teams is a passion of mine, and we started building our GM team from scratch. This was not a role I had envisioned when joining the company, though I took on the responsibility and relished the opportunity to do something I'd never done before.

Another invisible path presented itself when Volta's Chief People Officer resigned and I was asked to take over that position. The year 2022 was a period of growing crisis for the company, both financially and with executive turnover. Amidst this backdrop, I got the battlefield promotion to be the next head of the People team. This new role and path I hadn't expected was perhaps the hardest one of my professional career. Human Resources was never a role I had envisioned for myself and may not be in my future, but I sure learned a lot from this opportunity.

A common theme among these invisible paths at Volta was that being company-focused rather than functionally focused created unexpected journeys. My invisible paths opened up not only because I was a strong functional leader but also because I was a credible company leader and was pragmatic in working across functions. That mindset had been planted in me back in my time in the Marines, where we were taught the concept of combined arms. This ideal seeks to integrate different combat capabilities—infantry, artillery, armor, aviation, naval force—for complementary effects. You shouldn't just think about a mission or goal one-dimensionally. Rather, Marines plan and execute a mission with a comprehensive view of how to achieve it. Many civilian jobs, and the training that happens to get you there, are functionally focused. You have a job to do and are expected to develop narrow expertise to do it well. But once you get into leadership roles, it's important to look at each decision from a company-focused perspective. Understanding the combined-arms concept—and being able to apply it to Volta's challenges—made a big difference in how effective I was as a leader and in the opportunities that came to me as a result. I didn't always see the connection to my military experience but now realize there were a lot of invisible paths that appeared because of the leadership-development opportunities I was provided through what I learned as a Marine.

Whether personally or professionally, there is a path available to every one of us. This path isn't set in stone, and it may not be readily apparent; it is an invisible path, a path you can develop yourself.

Don't let the word *invisible* make you think there is some mystery to these paths that only presents itself to a select few. Countless individuals have gone on to achieve great success after taking a path that wasn't readily apparent to them.

Early in her career, Julia Child worked as a typist at the Office of Strategic Services (OSS), the forerunner to today's Central Intelligence Agency. It was 1942 and the height of World War II. At least twenty US Naval officers had been attacked by sharks since the start of the war, raising alarm among sailors and airmen who increasingly found themselves conducting dangerous missions on and over shark-infested waters. She soon found herself working in close proximity to OSS officers who were developing a shark repellent to help protect servicemen in the water. She helped the group experiment with different concoctions. They ultimately developed a recipe that was put into use. She continued to serve in the OSS until the end of the war and then moved to Paris with her husband. It was there she graduated from the famous Le Cordon Bleu cooking school in 1951 and began an illustrious career as a chef, author, and television personality.

Another example of taking the invisible path comes from space travel and American icon Sally Ride.

She was the first American woman, and youngest American ever, to have flown in space. Surely, someone who achieved such feats—she was just thirty-two when she first flew in space—had been planning and working toward that accomplishment from a very early age.

Not Sally Ride.

Ride grew up in Southern California and played tennis for the first time while on a family vacation in Europe at age nine. While she enjoyed many sports, tennis was her favorite. By age twelve, she was ranked in the top twenty for girls in Southern California in that age bracket. She continued enjoying sports in college at Swarthmore in Pennsylvania, playing golf, varsity field hockey, and becoming the Eastern Intercollegiate Women's Singles tennis champion. Ride moved back to California with the goal of becoming a professional tennis player.

She applied to transfer to Stanford University, ultimately earning an undergraduate degree in both physics and English literature. She then earned a master of science degree in physics in 1975 and a doctor of philosophy degree in 1978. Astrophysics and free-electron lasers were her areas of study.

While working on her PhD, Ride spotted an article in *The Stanford Daily* that told how the National Aeronautics and Space Administration

(NASA) was recruiting astronauts for the Space Shuttle program and was interested in female candidates. She was one of more than eight thousand initial applicants and was ultimately selected for the program.

She went on to be a part of two missions aboard the Space Shuttle and spent more than 340 days in space. After a planned third mission was canceled following the Challenger disaster in 1986, she left NASA the next year and took on a fellowship at Stanford; became a professor of physics at the University of California, San Diego; as well as a director of the California Space Institute (Cal Space), part of the university's Scripps Institution of Oceanography, among other things.

Sally Ride never set out to be an astronaut but followed a winding road that led to her making history and becoming a household name and inspiration to a generation of Americans.

Even with inspiration like those successful people, taking the leap and making that first step down an invisible path can be daunting. Why? Behavioral economics and psychology point us to one consideration. In 1979, Daniel Kahneman and his associate Amos Tversky coined the term *loss aversion* in their paper proposing an alternative model of decision-making in risky conditions. "The response to losses is stronger than the response to corresponding gains" is Kahneman's definition of loss aversion. "Losses loom larger than gains" implies that people by nature are averse to losses and tend to avoid them. Another way to think of this is succinctly stated in the old adage "A bird in the hand is worth two in the bush."

The prospect of taking an invisible path can lead to increased feelings of aversion to loss and us passing on a potentially lucrative path.

How, then, can we avoid this natural inclination to bypass these invisible opportunities?

Looking to others for inspiration is one way. Reading about and studying real-world examples of people overcoming tough circumstances, taking a chance, and achieving success can help make it easier to imagine yourself going after an unexpected opportunity and achieving success.

The way you frame an opportunity can significantly influence your perception of loss aversion. Thinking about an opportunity as a loss may increase loss aversion, while phrasing in your mind that same opportunity as a gain and highlighting the positive may reduce loss aversion, leading to a more calculated response. When a path appears, try framing the options in a way that highlights the potential benefits rather than emphasizing the risks.

It's also important to be honest about what could actually go wrong. Every decision and path doesn't always turn out positive, but thinking long term and putting a potential loss into perspective will help. If an immediate choice seems risky, and you live another fifty years after making that choice, that's a lot of time for that choice, and subsequent events, to play out. You will react to that choice over time, and that reaction can create incredible growth, and then that apparently risky choice will have had a good outcome.

Ask yourself what the worst outcome would be if the course of action was taken. This can help put loss, and the strong associated feelings associated with it, into perspective.

Finally, be mindful of hindsight bias and how it can impact your perception of the path you've taken. Hindsight bias is the belief, upon learning the outcome of an event, to overestimate one's ability to have foreseen that outcome. Whether it be an upset in a sporting event, an unforeseen run of good luck, or unplanned career choice or path, there is a tendency to tell ourselves, "I knew it all along."

That's just not true.

Life is a journey with no set path; this makes it an adventure and not simply a predetermined series of steps. There are many options, few markers, and no road signs. The worn paths may feel comfortable and safe. The invisible paths can be hard to find and fraught with pitfalls, missteps, and dead ends. It's those invisible paths, though, where opportunities arise and the adventure begins. Those invisible paths can begin with examining the delivery of a simple box.

If you want to be the best version of yourself, look for the invisible path.

CHAPTER THREE

Screwing Up Is Okay if You Recover Well

If you want to be the best version of yourself,
recognize when to admit your mistakes.

NO MATTER HOW BAD THINGS MAY SEEM, they can always be worse. I regularly say to my sons when confronted with a seemingly significant (but in reality minor) setback, "If this is the worst thing that happens to us today, we are going to be just fine." At the same time, it's important to know and accept when something has gone very wrong and action needs to be taken. I learned this lesson well toward the end of the first week at OCS.

Ranks in the Marines are divided into two broad categories, officers and enlisted. Commissioned officers start as second lieutenants and then move on to first lieutenant, captain, major, lieutenant colonel, colonel, and finally four different levels of general.

Enlisted Marines begin with the rank of private, then advance to private first class and lance corporal; these are often referred to collectively as junior enlisted. The next ranks are corporals and sergeants, and Marines in those ranks are known as non-commissioned officers (NCO). They take on a great deal of responsibility and hold a special position as leaders among Marines. The third and final grouping of the enlisted ranks is staff non-commissioned officers. These include staff sergeants, gunnery sergeants, first sergeants, master sergeants, sergeants major, and master gunnery sergeants.

By definition, all officers are senior to enlisted Marines. You could have been sworn in as a second lieutenant five minutes ago, and a sergeant major with twenty-five years in the Corps would salute you in respect to your rank. While officers may be senior on paper, it's well understood that Staff NCOs hold a special position and responsibility in the Marines. When a Staff NCO says something, everyone, regardless of rank, listens. A smart second lieutenant will listen. Colonels listen. Generals definitely listen.

The importance of Staff NCOs was impressed upon us from the very beginning of OCS and only increased as our training progressed. Candidates spend nearly their entire day under the watchful eye of three staff sergeants, the senior one referred to as the platoon sergeant. Platoon Sergeants train you, push your limits, berate you, discipline you, and pretty much control all aspects of your life for the ten weeks of OCS.

When the platoon sergeant calls you to his office, a few thoughts immediately go through your head. *Oh no. Why is he calling me? Please, let me make sure I don't screw this up and draw more attention to myself.*

No candidate wants to have any more facetime with their platoon sergeant than absolutely necessary. A one-on-one in their office is even worse. The best approach was to get in, get whatever they have on their mind over with, and get out of there as soon as you could.

That's what I was faced with toward the end of my few days as our platoon's first candidate platoon sergeant. I'm sure there was a question I didn't have the answer to, some colorful feedback about why one of the other candidates was late to muster that morning, or why I was having trouble marching the platoon the proper way.

Just need to make it through this meeting and then lunch, and then a new candidate will rotate into this position, and I can try to be low profile for a while.

I mentally walked through the proper procedure as I approached the office. First, come to the position of attention outside the door. Then, close your fist and bang loudly on the door frame three times to announce your presence. Finally, sound off loudly with, "Candidate Platoon Sergeant Michaels reporting as ordered!"

Coming to the position of attention was easy, but it went downhill from there. I made a fist and banged three times but was not paying attention, and instead of banging on the solid metal door frame, my fist hit the wall just to the side. The wall where a framed glass picture was hanging. A framed picture of a rhinoceros that was gifted to our platoon sergeant years ago as his face—and demeanor—had a striking resemblance to that beast. He had taken the nickname "Rhino" and had hung this gift in his office. My fist had just brought it smashing down to the waxed tile floor in a thousand shards.

There was a moment of silence. I tried to maintain my bearing and keep my eyes facing forward. It was hard, though, to not peek around and see the broken glass and picture frame, as well as the now destroyed picture of the rhino on the floor. That silence didn't last long.

The staff at OCS had stopped swearing years prior. The training to be an officer was serious business, and it was culturally important for the enlisted platoon sergeants to set an example for the soon-to-be officers they were training. So, there were no f-bombs barked that day, but my platoon sergeant still lit into me like there was no tomorrow. I thought about uttering something in response but was in shock, and with his face one inch in front of mine and the intensity of his voice, I could tell this was not a time he wanted to hear more from me. He closed with a loud,

"Get OUT of my office!" and I quickly about-faced and double-timed back to my rack.

Lots of thoughts can go through your head after an event like that. The first one that came to mind was, *They are going to send me home, and I haven't even been here a week.*

I tried to focus the remainder of that afternoon as we marched, climbed, polished our boots, and cleaned our rifles. All I could think of was that I would soon be heading home, this little experiment of mine in the Marines having proved a short-lived failure. *If I'm heading home, I should at least give the platoon sergeant a formal apology and walk out with my head held high.*

Again, no one wants to have a one-on-one conversation with their platoon sergeant any more than they have to. Even trying to find a time to speak with him wasn't easy. I found my moment, though, as the rest of the platoon was assembling outside so the new candidate platoon sergeant could march them to dinner. I hung back in the squad bay and cautiously approached him.

"Platoon Sergeant, Candidate Michaels requests permission to speak."

He didn't say yes, as much as he squinted his eyes in what seemed to be a willingness to hear me.

"Platoon Sergeant, Candidate Michaels would like to apologize for what happened earlier. I'm sorry. I recognize I did not follow the proper procedure earlier and knocked on the wall instead of the door frame. I did not intend to break your framed picture, and I'd like to pay to have it replaced as soon as I'm able."

The interaction was only seconds long, but it felt like an eternity. His intense eyes peered into mine. And then he briefly said in a gruff but subdued voice, "No. That's not necessary. Now get back with the platoon right now."

He didn't have to tell me twice. I hastened to meet up with the rest of the platoon.

I can't tell you what was going through his head, either earlier that afternoon or just at that moment. He might have expected it and he might not have, but I'd like to think he respected me for coming back to apologize.

I've made other mistakes since then, and I have to admit that some have been easier to accept than others. Why? Some mistakes and failures are small and readily reversible, while others have longer-lasting impacts. Some mistakes are private, and it can be easier to admit those to yourself, while others are public and entail admitting failure in front of others.

No one enjoys being wrong, and we all react to it in different ways. Some of us admit we were wrong, while others might imply they were wrong-ish but don't do so explicitly or in a way that clearly admits fault. Still others may flat out refuse to admit a mistake, even in the face of overwhelming evidence, so we double down rather than face the truth. Our confirmation bias might kick in, causing us to seek out evidence to prove what we already believe ... the car you cut off has a small dent in its bumper, which obviously means that person isn't a good driver, and the little altercation you just had is clearly the other driver's fault.

Psychologists call this cognitive dissonance. We experience stress and mental anguish when we try to hold two contradictory thoughts, beliefs, opinions, or attitudes at the same time. For example, you might believe you are a kind person, so when you rudely bump into someone on the sidewalk and don't immediately apologize, you experience dissonance. That is an unpleasant mental state our minds try to avoid. To cope with it, you deny your mistake and insist the other person should have seen you first, or that you had the right of way even if you didn't.

Recognizing this cognitive dissonance is one thing. But how do we get past it?

Start with recognizing cognitive dissonance when it presents itself. Your mind will naturally try to preserve your sense of identity and how that has developed over time, so be aware of what that dissonance feels like in real time. It can often manifest itself as confusion, stress, embarrassment, or guilt. None of these necessarily mean you are in the wrong, but if you can at least recognize them, you can use them as reminders to explore the situation from an impartial perspective and objectively question whether you are at fault.

At the same time, learn to recognize how your mind normally works . . . your usual justifications and rationalizations. When were you wrong and knew it but tried to justify it somehow? Remember how it felt to rationalize your behavior, and pinpoint that feeling as cognitive dissonance the next time it happens.

Finally, remember that people are often more forgiving than you might think. What we might perceive internally as an insurmountable mistake isn't often perceived as significantly by others. Traits like honesty and humility make you more human and therefore more relatable.

Was my platoon sergeant going to send me home for this error and end my military career before it ever really got started? Did he feel differently about me after I approached him to apologize? Hard to say, and I'll never know for sure. What I do know is that I did the right thing. I was proud of mustering the courage to seek another interaction with him (and possibly incurring even more of his wrath) and taking the harder path of admitting my mistake and apologizing for it. I'd like to think he respected me for it, and at a minimum I was able to hold my head high for the remainder of OCS. While the remaining weeks were no cakewalk, I was able to continue and graduate and ultimately spend ten years as a leader of Marines. Don't try to break the glass-framed picture of the rhino . . . but if you do, own up to it.

If you want to be the best version of yourself, recognize when to admit your mistakes.

CHAPTER FOUR

Say Yes

If you want to be the best version of yourself,
know that you are more ready than you think.

THE *TOP GUN* MOVIES AND ICONIC LEAD
character Maverick have entered the collective consciousness of American
society thanks to Tom Cruise. While Maverick is a fictional character,
Top Gun does exist and is more formally known within the Navy as
Naval Fighter Weapons School. That doesn't roll off the tongue quite as
easily as Top Gun, and that's what many Americans will recognize if it is
mentioned in conversation.

There is a similar school and top-level designation for helicopter
pilots, albeit with not as quite a Hollywood-ready name: Weapons and
Tactics Instructor (WTI). Being invited to the WTI program is an honor,
and only a select few in the helicopter community are able to attend and
graduate from that course.

It's six weeks of intensive studying and flying. The first three weeks
are classroom based, with academic topics that include enemy weapons
systems, flight tactics, and methodologies for planning and leading large-
scale missions. The following three weeks are a series of missions that esca-
late in size and complexity, encompassing dozens of aircraft of different
types, as well as coordination with ground units and other aspects of the
most complex missions Marines undertake.

Graduates of WTI are recognized as the best tacticians and pilots
the Marines have. They are the ones the commanding officer (CO) looks
to when it comes to handling the training plan for the entire squadron.
They are the ones the CO looks to when they need to hear, "We're good

to go into combat." It can be a launch pad to a long and successful career as helicopter pilot.

I remember the day when my CO informed me I had been selected from my squadron to attend WTI. I had the chance to fly with the best helicopter pilots the Marines had. I turned it down.

Why would someone do that? Why, given the chance to learn and fly with the best, would an ambitious pilot say no?

After completing OCS, The Basic School, and Flight School, I arrived at my first fleet squadron, the Flying Tigers of Marine Heavy Helicopter Squadron 361, and found out we were soon to start a year-long deployment cycle. A portion of the squadron would separate and join a reinforced squadron of multiple aircraft types that would become the Air Combat Element of a Marine Expeditionary Unit (Special Operations Capable), or MEU(SOC). It was the prestigious route to take. Cool missions, lots of flying. Other pilots in the squadron would spend time on a shorter deployment cycle where there wasn't as much flying, or spend six months land based in Okinawa. Not a lot of great flying happening in Okinawa. I seized that opportunity and had an amazing next year as a pilot as part of that MEU(SOC). There were six months of work ups preparing for the deployment and then six months aboard a Navy amphibious assault ship deployed across the Pacific and to the Arabian Gulf. I earned my first big designation on that cruise, helicopter aircraft commander, and was on a fast track to section leader, division leader, night systems instructor, and other advanced designations.

After returning from that first deployment, there would be a year of operating out of our home base, Miramar, with many trainings and missions conducted on a regular basis. At the end of that year we would start another year-long MEU(SOC) cycle that included a six-month workup and six-month deployment. During that interim year, there was a WTI class, and our squadron was able to send a pilot. My commanding officer called me to his office one day and informed me he wanted to nominate me for that spot. This was a coveted offer that few received to a prestigious school. It would put me on the fast track for even more flight time and opportunities.

I told him I wanted to think about it. No doubt that response surprised him.

That first deployment, while enjoyable, was also eye-opening for me. There were other WTIs in our squadron, and I couldn't help but be impressed with their level of professionalism and flying skills. They were really good. *Could I fly like that someday? Could I lead a mission of the size and complexity they seemed to do with ease?* While I saw myself on a path to being like them, I thought I would need a few more years of experience before I could lead large-scale missions the way they did.

The next few days were personally challenging as I labored to consider the opportunity in front of me.

Do I reach beyond what I'm comfortable with and take this?
Do I sit back and stay with what is comfortable?
This could be what really helps my piloting career take off.
I don't think I'm ready for this.

I went back to the CO's office a few days later after struggling with what I wanted to do and what I wanted to achieve. I told him I was thankful for the opportunity but didn't want to take it. He was taken aback, and after some follow-on conversations over the next few weeks, another pilot went to WTI and represented our squadron.

The funny thing about it was that I ended up going to WTI anyway, albeit not as a pilot. The training program was in need of an officer to support the course on a short-term basis, and this time I didn't have a choice. I attended the first three weeks and completed the academic portion and then spent the next three weeks assisting with administrative scheduling work and monitoring the radios back on the ground in the ready room. I heard the missions as they were assigned, watched the planning process, and learned from the pre- and post-flight briefings. All from the comfort of my chair.

I walked away at the end of those three weeks thinking, *Damn, I can do everything those pilots can. I could now be a graduate of WTI.*

I continued flying and had the opportunity to continue to progress but never became a WTI. I had the chance to attend a prestigious aviation school and receive training only a few do, and I passed it up. Twenty-five years later I still think about that missed opportunity. Someone thought I was ready to take a big step in my career, but I didn't see it in myself at the time.

Why would someone pass up a great opportunity for professional development and the ensuing opportunities that come from it? One place we can look for answers is the field of psychology and the Dunning-Kruger effect, published by David Dunning and Justin Kruger in 1999. Simply put, this cognitive bias describes how people with limited competence in a particular domain overestimate their abilities. The theory also suggests an opposite effect for high performers: A tendency to underestimate their skills. *Was I underestimating my skills?*

These tendencies for unskilled individuals to overestimate their own ability and the tendency for experts to underestimate their own abilities have been questioned. Not all researchers agree on the magnitude of the effect, so let's not put too much significance on this. Rather, a key point is that while too much confidence can be bad, not enough confidence at the right moment is a real possibility and can be even worse.

Where else can we look in trying to understand the mentality of those who have taken advantage of opportunities that presented themselves? One example is former President Barack Obama. During his keynote speech at the 2004 Democratic National Convention, Obama introduced himself as a skinny kid with a funny name. His speech was well received and elevated his status within the Democratic Party. He was elected to the US Senate three months later. A transformative political career was launched when he initiated what was considered a long-shot bid for the presidency. A moment presented itself, and Obama seized that moment.

We could also highlight Volodymyr Zelensky, a former comedian and actor who was elected the sixth president of Ukraine in 2019. When Russia invaded Ukraine in February 2022, his leadership during the crisis won him widespread international praise, and he has been lauded as a symbol of the Ukrainian resistance. Zelensky was named the *Time* Person of the Year for 2022. He was tested in a moment and seized the opportunity to demonstrate his leadership, not taking the offer to evacuate the country that was presented to him.

Taylor Swift, perhaps the greatest entertainer of this generation, is another who seized a moment that was presented to her and has never looked back. While promoting her self-titled debut studio album in 2006, Swift was making the rounds of local country music radio stations. As legend has it, on the way to K-FROG Radio in Riverside, California,

Swift sat in the back of the car strumming through her first single, "Tim McGraw," when her manager told her he was warned by the station not to ask the busy program directors to put her on the air. When Swift, playing the song in the station's studio, got to the line in "Tim McGraw" that includes the lyric "someday you'll turn your radio on," she glanced over at the assembled men in the room and instead sang "someday you'll turn K-FROG on." She had but a fleeting moment to make a decision, and she said yes and took it. The gimmick worked. The station immediately wanted to put her on the radio. "Tim McGraw" was Swift's first chart entry in the United States: it peaked at number forty on the *Billboard* Hot 100 at the time and later was ranked by *Rolling Stone* at number eleven on its "The 100 Greatest Debut Singles of All Time" list. Swift built on that early win and has continued to build a music and entertainment juggernaut second to none.

Those are all examples of famous people, you say. They had a lot going for them when their moment presented itself; of course they were successful. There have been many others who are not household names yet were ready for a big step in their career and seized the opportunity presented to them. An example from the world of sports is Jeremy Lin, an undersized and undrafted basketball player from Harvard. He was waived by two teams in the 2011 season before getting a roster spot as a point guard with the New York Knicks the next year. Lin was sleeping on a family member's couch, underappreciated by his teammates, not getting playing time, and on the verge of being cut from the team when his moment of opportunity came. He was promoted to the starting lineup after the Knicks went through a stretch of losing eleven out of thirteen games and had multiple other players sidelined due to injuries.

In that first game he put up twenty-five points, dished out seven assists, and grabbed five rebounds while he led his team to the win. He put up twenty-eight points in the next game and twenty-three in the one after that as the Knicks took off on a winning streak led by Lin. Continuing to seize the moment, Lin took the world by storm after scoring thirty-eight points against the legendary Kobe Bryant and the Lakers. *Thirty-eight points against Kobe at a sold-out Madison Square Garden?!* Two nights later, on the road against the Toronto Raptors, Lin had the ball near half court, with his team down and fourteen seconds left in the game. His teammates were motioning for him to pass to them or set up a pick-and-roll. Lin waved them off. He motioned for them to get out of his way, as if saying, *I deserve to be here, too.* With confidence in his game and knowing this opportunity might never come along again, Lin took the final shot and nailed it with less than a second to go to win the game. The fairy tale run continued, and the Knicks ultimately made the playoffs, while Lin appeared on the covers of *Sports Illustrated* and *Time* and was named to the *Time* 100 as one of the most influential people in the world. In July 2012, Lin won the ESPY Award for Breakthrough Athlete of the Year. While his career never again had the highs of Linsanity that captivated the sports world in 2012, he won a championship in 2019 as part of an NBA career that spanned nine years. When you get that opportunity, you have to kick the door in . . . Lin not only kicked it in, he blew it up.

My message here is not to compare myself to others or try to draw comparisons with famous and accomplished professionals. Rather, it is to look at the preceding examples as models of how an individual can see that an opportunity is presenting itself and seize the moment to achieve great things.

It's also important to be aware that there is a danger of getting too caught up in a counterfactual. A counterfactual is what might have been—an imaginary alternative to the actual past. One could create a new narrative of how much better off—or maybe worse off—you would be now if you had made a different decision back then. Had I attended WTI, one counterfactual I could envision was to decide to stay in the Marines for a career, perhaps have multiple overseas assignments and live around the world, maybe even have a distinguished career and rise to the rank of general. Who knows? You can beat yourself up unnecessarily thinking too much about what could have been, and that's not healthy or helpful. Rather, recognize when a significant opportunity comes your way and have a predisposition to say yes.

Please understand that saying yes doesn't mean saying yes to every little thing that comes along, every favor asked of you, and every request sent your way. Rather, saying yes as I intend it means to see those big, hairy opportunities as they arise and recognize the moment. Don't shy away from those moments. Take them. It's not easy to know when one of those potentially meaningful opportunities is happening, but have faith in your intuition, yourself, and your abilities. Take them head on. Those are the moments that can shape the trajectory of your personal and professional life.

A final perspective comes from someone most consider the National Football League (NFL) GOAT, the greatest of all time, Tom Brady. Brady spoke in a 2023 interview about his approach to gaining success as a rookie in the NFL. His perspective as a seven-time Super Bowl champion on what it was like when he was new in the league is invaluable.

After getting drafted by the New England Patriots, Brady entered training camp as the 199th pick with incredibly low expectations and found himself getting just two practice reps at a time. Meanwhile, the starter was getting twenty team reps while the backup quarterback was getting about ten.

Brady asked, "How can I ever get better? All these guys get all the reps."

He was then advised, "Just go in there and focus with the two that you got and make them as perfect as you possibly can."

And that's what he did. The coaches put him in for his two reps and Brady "sprinted in like it was the Super Bowl."

"And I did really well with those two because I brought enthusiasm, I brought some energy, and I had a little more confidence in myself. It went from getting two reps to getting four reps because those two were pretty good. Then I had four good reps. Then I had ten good reps."

Through this new attitude, he focused on what he could control.

"Whenever you get an opportunity, you take advantage of it, you treat it like it's the Super Bowl. You treat it like it's game day. Go out there and treat practice like no one else does. And I did that every single day."

The rest, as they say, is history. He said yes and achieved amazing things.

In the decades since I turned down the opportunity to attend WTI, I continue to think about that missed chance and the opportunity I passed up for not a great reason. I wish I had that one back. I wish I had said yes like Obama, Zelensky, Swift, Lin, and Brady did when they got their chance.

If you want to be the best version of yourself, say yes and take advantage of meaningful opportunities when they arise.

CHAPTER FIVE

This Is the Business
We Have Chosen

If you want to be the best version of yourself,
own your choices.

THE GENERAL FINALLY CALLED US INTO
his office. I was standing with my co-pilot to one side, and then the squadron executive officer (XO), squadron CO, and group CO to the other. All of us standing tall at the position of attention in front of The Man. Not a place anyone wants to ever be.

How did I get here? How did I get a major, lieutenant colonel, and bird colonel in this position, about to all get their asses chewed by a two-star general?

Allow me to rewind a few hours and tell you how the day started...

What a day to fly! The morning fog was clearing over the Southern California coast, and blue skies were breaking through. The ready room was alive with activity as pilots from our squadron were conducting their mission briefs for flights to occur later that day. My copilot for the day, another captain, was senior to me, but I was the assigned aircraft commander that day and responsible for our fast-roping mission with Marines up the coast at Camp Pendleton's Combat Town. It was the summer of 1999, and I was a newly minted aircraft commander, just back from my first overseas deployment and eager to continue my progression as a helicopter pilot.

Combat Town is pretty much what it sounds like: A collection of cinder-block structures a few stories tall laid out like a couple of typical city blocks. It's used by Marines to simulate combat situations and practice maneuvering around streets in an urban area, as well as to practice clearing buildings. For the latter, imagine a three- or four-story building with enemy combatants in different rooms across multiple floors. For our fast-roping mission, we would fly at a high speed from a concealed position into Combat Town, execute a quick stop, and come to a hover over the top of the target building. Our crew chief would then deploy the fast rope from the center of our helo, and the Marines would slide down the rope to the rooftop (bless those Marines for the things they do). Once they were all on the roof, the helicopter would accelerate away, and they would conduct their mission to clear the building.

We met the ground unit near Combat Town and conducted our mission brief. We started executing immediately after. The first few cycles went well. My quick stops were aggressive but smooth (if I may say so myself). The quick stop maneuver is much like it sounds . . . we approached the target building at a high speed and flared the nose of the aircraft up while reducing power; that slowed the aircraft's speed quickly. Then we came back to a hovering position directly over the top of the building. An observer would say that maneuver, when properly executed, looked a bit unusual and perhaps like something was going wrong, as the nose of the helo would be raised to what seemed to be an excessive angle toward the sky, but that was intended and needed to quickly bleed off airspeed. We can agree that I was performing some aggressive quick stops that day. Damn, were they good!

Maybe too good, as what happened next highlighted the aggressiveness of my flying and the perception an outside observer had of my technique and the extent to which he thought I was maneuvering the aircraft and flaring the nose of the helo to an unnatural (and potentially unsafe) angle.

We landed after completing our fourth insertion of the Marines to their rooftop destination to pick them up and start another cycle. At that moment, the radio crackled to life.

"Aircraft operating at Combat Town, identify yourself."

Huh. I wonder who he is talking to.

I looked around the area and saw no other aircraft anywhere nearby.

Huh. He is talking to me.

I responded with my callsign, "This is Tiger 16."

"Tiger 16, this is General DeLong. I've been watching you. I don't like what I've seen. Come see me as soon as you return to base."

Oh shit.

Pilots use the term *compartmentalization* to refer to how, when in the cockpit, you have to block out thoughts about family, finances, your plans for the upcoming weekend, as well as everything else, and focus solely on the task at hand. Well, I just had a two-star general—the wing commanding general—who happened to be in another aircraft nearby, call me out. I compartmentalized as best I could as we finished the mission. As we flew back to Miramar, I couldn't help wondering what was going to happen when we landed.

It didn't take long to find out.

"What the hell did you do?" Our squadron XO was standing at the entrance to the hangar as we walked back after shutting down on the flight line. The first sentence out of his mouth and the tone with which it was delivered told me that word traveled fast, he was clearly upset, and the rest of this afternoon was not going to go well.

It seems the general thought my flying that day was overly and unnecessarily aggressive for a training mission and intended to formally reprimand me in front of my entire chain of command to demonstrate how upset and serious he was.

The XO proceeded to tell me he had dispatched a half dozen lieutenants to scour the base to find our squadron CO so we could all head to the general's office for this special meeting with him.

We arrived at Wing headquarters not long after and saw our squadron CO, a lieutenant colonel, waiting for us. Standing next to him was our group CO, a full-bird colonel, Colonel McNamara. (Note: a lieutenant colonel is sometimes referred to as a light colonel, while the next rank higher, colonel, is often referred to as a bird colonel as a means of distinction by using the ranks' insignia, which looks like an eagle with its head to one side, as a differentiating factor.)

To put this military lineup into a civilian perspective, this is the equivalent to being a manager at a company (me) and having your chief operating officer (the squadron XO), your chief executive officer (the squadron CO), and the CEO of their parent company (the group CO), all stand in front of the CEO of their parent company (the wing commanding general), who is essentially the CEO of a Fortune 500 company. Not a place anyone wants to ever be.

Ooh. This is getting more serious, fast.

There may have been a brief pleasantry or two exchanged between those senior officers, but I must have missed it as we started walking into Wing Headquarters. We were met by the general's chief of staff, who escorted us into an anteroom outside his office.

As my (bad) luck would have it, the general was occupied with some calls and visitors about a developing issue in real time; there was an F/A-18 Hornet circling over Miramar with stuck landing gear. Since the gear would not fully deploy to allow for a safe landing, the pilot was preparing to dump fuel to minimize the risk of a catastrophic mishap if he ultimately needed to land on the runway without all his gear down and safely locked in place. With this situation rapidly evolving, an ever-growing group was assembling at Wing Headquarters to monitor progress and brief the general.

The general finally called us into his office. There we were: my copilot and I, and then the major, lieutenant colonel, and colonel standing tall at the position of attention in front of The Man.

The general started speaking. While there were five of us in front of him, his words and scowl were clearly directed at me. He was firm in his tone, but it wasn't quite as bad as I had prepared myself for.

I may make it out of this okay. Maybe just be grounded from flying for a few days.

As he paced back and forth in front of us, he paused momentarily. Then the general's voice gradually grew louder and his tone stronger. This was no longer a mild scolding . . . it had turned into a full on ass-chewing of yours truly in front of what was now a crowd of dozens of other assembled officers in the anteroom just steps away.

It may be a cliche to say an event that lasts just a minute can feel like an eternity, but that doesn't make it any less true in a situation like this. As I stood at the position of attention for that eternity, with my entire chain of command right next to me, all I could think was that this was going so badly that the next thing that was going to happen was that he was going to take my wings from me, and I'd be spending the rest of my time as a Marine flying a desk.

The general finished his dressing down (and didn't take my wings!) and rapidly dismissed us from this office. We exited past the growing crowd in the anteroom, as that F/A-18 was still circling overhead with a potential mishap brewing, and walked outside. I can only imagine the look on my face; some combination of fear, relief, disbelief, and utter shock at having experienced something most pilots never will.

Colonel McNamara looked at me as a slight smile grew from the corner of his mouth. "You realize, Captain, what happened in there?"

"No, Sir."

"He made an example of you. He started somewhat mildly, and his tone changed as he realized there was an audience right outside that could see and hear everything he was saying. See, this Wing has one of the worst safety records in the Marines, and with that F/A-18 issue happening right now, there is yet another potential mishap that is going to go on the general's record. He realized he had an audience of squadron COs and other senior officers from across the Wing gathered outside. What better way to make an impression on them than to have them watch a young captain get his ass chewed? Imagine what they all will report back to their squadrons about what they observed and how serious the general is about safety."

The explanation made sense, though I suspect my face still displayed some unusual combination of emotions. Sensing this, the colonel continued.

"You ever watch *The Godfather*? The second one? You know that scene where Michael Corleone is confronting Hyman Roth about the death of Frank Pentangeli? Hyman Roth then turns the table on Michael and talks about his good friend Moe Greene."

I must have still had that confused look on my face.

The colonel continued, "Hyman says, 'Someone put a bullet through his eye. No one knows who gave the order. When I heard it, I wasn't angry. I knew Moe, I knew he was headstrong. Talking loud, saying stupid things. So when he turned up dead, I let it go. And I said to myself, 'This is the business we've chosen.' Basically, Hyman is telling Michael he knows Michael had his friend Moe killed, and Hyman didn't take revenge or further action. He let it go. It was business, and the business—the mafia—the two of them had chosen."

"Well, there, Captain, this is the business you have chosen. You have chosen to be a Marine aviator. You chose to be a helicopter pilot. You chose to fly the way you did. You made these choices. This is what happens when you fly helicopters. Things like this are going to happen. There will be run-ins with senior officers. Don't like it? Don't want it? You are in the wrong business. This is the business you have chosen."

Those words sank in for a minute. Ready to be done with conversations with senior officers for the day, I saluted, about-faced, and headed back to our squadron. *This is the business I have chosen.*

There were quite a few questions about the day's events when I got back to our squadron ready room. After sharing the story with my fellow pilots, the phone rang. The officer on duty picked up, said, "Yes, sir. He's right here," and handed me the phone. It was Colonel McNamara. I wasn't quite sure what to expect and certainly didn't think he would be calling me only twenty minutes after being part of that meeting in the general's office.

"How you doing, Captain? I wanted to call and share something. After you left I went back and spoke with the general again. See, he and I have known each other for a long time. I was a lieutenant when he was a captain, and we were in the same squadron back in the Vietnam days. I told him he should be happy with you."

"Uh, how's that, Sir?"

"I told the general he should be happy to have pilots in his Wing that can fly like that, like you did today. The general? Well, he grunted and said, 'Perhaps you are right.' So that's that. Keep your head high, Captain, and remember what I told you."

That was twenty-five years ago. I think of that day regularly and have told that story (I try to abbreviate it) to many coworkers in a variety of different situations. The big takeaway is quite simple: Whatever you are doing, it's the business you have chosen. You made a conscious decision as an adult, and there is no blame or bad feelings to be passed to another. Working at a series-B startup and it's crazy as hell? You joined start-up-world, and this is the business you have chosen. Decided to take a new role and you weren't sure exactly how it would play out? You took a chance, and this is the business you have chosen. No need to get frustrated or mopey or despondent about it. There is no one to blame but yourself, because this is the business you have chosen. Get your butt back up, run to the sound of the guns, and get back in the fight.

The other takeaway was that follow-up phone call from the colonel to try to cheer up a young captain at the end of the day. He didn't need to, but he did. He made the time to call a young officer who was feeling shell-shocked and gave him the morale boost he needed. That's leadership.

If you want to be the best version of yourself, own your choices.

CHAPTER SIX

Set a North Star

*If you want to be the best version of yourself,
set clear expectations with yourself and with others,
documenting them clearly and succinctly.*

AS WE START TO EXPLORE THE IMPOR-
tance of setting a North Star, this chapter begins by taking a step back
chronologically from where the prior chapter ended. We rewind a few
years to TBS and meet my platoon commander, Captain Jones. We then
move ahead a few years to an operational squadron led by Lieutenant
Colonel Reinecke. That foundational, early Marines experience with
Captain Jones is complemented by a similar perspective years later with
Lieutenant Colonel Reinecke. They combine to become a perfect example of setting clear expectations.

A platoon is a core component of Marine infantry units. With
that, Officer Candidate School is structured around platoons. Each platoon has a platoon commander who oversees training and the work of
the platoon sergeant. Those platoon commanders, usually captains, are
important, though it's the enlisted platoon sergeants, usually holding the
rank of staff sergeant, who perform the majority of the instruction with
officer candidates.

Less well-known, though perhaps more important, is what comes
after graduating OCS: The Basis School (TBS). While OCS is ten weeks
long and serves the important role of determining who has the strength,
fortitude, and raw leadership ability to become an officer, TBS is truly
where second lieutenants are trained and developed. TBS is an intensive,
six-month-long school that instructs every officer, regardless of what their
specialty will be, in how to be an infantry platoon commander. Patrols.

Land navigation. Ambushes. Establishing defensive perimeters. A lieutenant will have to pass all these areas to graduate, and only then will they head to their dedicated school for their assigned specialty and finally on to an operational unit. You want to be in a combat arms role? You have to make it through TBS first. Want to be a pilot? Have to graduate from TBS first. Destined to be a lawyer? Not until after TBS.

So, while enlisted platoon sergeants are the primary drivers at OCS, it's the captains and majors who are the primary instructors and role models at TBS. The best way to learn how to be an officer is to spend as much time as you can around one.

Thus began my six months at TBS and time in 4th Platoon with Captain Robert Jones. He was every bit the infantry Marine you could imagine. High and tight hair. Solid, muscular build. Slightly raspy voice. Squinty eyes. This was a Marine to learn from.

We had a formation that first day, and Captain Jones laid out his expectations for our platoon of forty lieutenants. He spoke about his experience leading Marines and what it was like to be an officer in a fleet unit. He shared his experiences training Marines and helping them with professional and personal issues. While we realized it was expected of an officer to train a young Marine in the art of combat, it came as a surprise to us when he informed us that we could be called on to help a Marine with a family problem, or help them buy a car. As junior officers, we would be expected to help the Marines in our units with any number of issues that might come up. The assembled platoon stood in formation and listened and learned. It was a lot to take in, and he knew it.

To help us internalize and remember the main concepts of that meeting, Captain Jones followed by issuing each of us a two-sided document (that I still have to this day) that succinctly summarized what he had just told us. While it started with the somewhat bland subject line of "Policy letter," the first paragraph clearly set the tone for what he was about to document: "In this letter I will establish general guidelines for the officers in the platoon to follow. I will also outline my personal philosophy on leadership."

From there, he broke his comments into clear areas: What to Expect of Me and My Expectations of You. As with his spoken words, the simplicity of his writing was genius.

His explanation of what we should expect of him was perfectly clear and succinct. "I am both your teacher and evaluator. I will participate in all phases of your training and will instruct many of your classes. My job is to teach you how to be Marine officers, and the best way to do that is by example. You will learn to do things the right way, and I will hold you to the highest standards. You will be treated like company-grade officers unless you deserve otherwise."

In referring to us as company-grade officers (a grouping that includes second lieutenants, first lieutenants, and captains), he was signaling that the yelling and screaming of OCS was over, and that while we would still need to refer to him as "Sir" and salute accordingly, we were going to have a different kind of relationship with him than we did with the platoon sergeants at OCS.

Equally clear and thoughtful were his expectations of us. "In six short months you could be leading Marines in combat. Give 110 percent at all times, and pursue your professional education with a ferocious desire. Be aggressive, proactive, and team-oriented at all times. Effective leaders are not passive. Be a positive force even when in a follower's role.

Leadership is displayed on a daily basis and is not measured solely on the rare occasion that you hold a formal billet. Strive to consistently display motivation, cooperation, and a willingness to be part of the solution. When in charge—LEAD! If you make a mistake, make an aggressive mistake in the spirit of trying to do what is right."

The next paragraph was equally pithy: "If you are ever in doubt, follow the Three Rules: always do what is right, never assume anyone knows anything unless you tell them, and never miss an opportunity to keep your mouth shut (especially in front of a general officer)."

He concluded on the back page with his philosophy of command. There were a dozen points that were all extremely relevant and important, and nearly thirty years later these four are as relevant as ever:

- The standards we set will be higher than those of anyone evaluating us.

- The policies of the unit are set by the commander. All input and suggestions are welcome, but when decisions are made, the time for talking is over—it is time to execute.

- Two characteristics that will mark this unit and set us apart from our contemporaries: Intelligent, efficient planning, and ruthless, ferocious execution.

- This unit exists to win and fight on the battlefield. Everything we do must ultimately contribute to that goal.

After graduating from TBS, I moved to other units in the Marines. One commanding officer was especially impactful in the expectations he set with the squadrons he commanded: Lieutenant Colonel Rich Reinecke, call sign Lobo. Lobo was lean and wiry, and while he didn't have the linebacker-like build one often associates with Marines, he was one of the finest leaders I worked under.

As we started our first combined-training exercises with the ground and naval forces that would be part of the 11th MEU(SOC) aboard the USS Boxer in the fall of 2000, it was Lobo who volunteered to be the Air Mission Commander (AMC) for the first joint mission we performed. This was a large and daunting role, and Lobo could have easily assigned one of his captains or majors to serve as the AMC and lead the mission. But no, Lobo was not about to ask any officers to later do something that he had not first done himself.

Later on that deployment, Lobo spoke to the officers one evening to share his thoughts and observations about his time as a Marine. He was coming toward the end of his time in the Corps and wanted to share with us younger officers what he had learned from more than twenty years in uniform. He spoke about a lot that evening, and a poignant message was his personal leadership philosophy that he had developed over the prior decades. His medium was a PowerPoint presentation, and the black words on that simple white background struck me in their simplicity. There were three key points: Know your stuff, take care of your Marines, do the right thing. Much like with Captain Jones, the simplicity of the words was a big part of what made them so powerful.

Lobo's words stayed with me the following years as I finished my time in the Marines, went to graduate school, and started my civilian career. Recall the fall of 2008 when I joined EnerNOC as an individual contributor project manager and then was promoted to a management position and would be leading the field operations team. They were a great team of project managers and site technicians, and I wanted to set expectations soon after taking over regarding how we could continue to excel as a team.

While I had what I believed was a strong leadership ethos, I had never actually written it down. It was time to put pen to paper and take all those ideas that had been part of my beliefs and actions and take the next step of committing them to paper. Writing succinctly and committing words to paper forces clarity of thought, and there is no stronger way to share your beliefs than to document and share them widely, just as Captain Jones and Lieutenant Colonel Reinecke had years before.

I wrote a one-page Expectations document that addressed three main areas: What I expected of individuals on my team, what they could expect of me, and how we would be successful together. I couldn't help but be guided by the expectations Captain Jones had set for the young officers in his platoon decades earlier. With every new member of my team, we sat down before lunch on their first day and discussed that piece of paper I handed them.

This document evolved over the years as my roles changed and my leadership approach continued to evolve. I have continuously drawn on my experiences managing managers, building new teams, and continuing to read and learn from other great leaders. Lobo's words continued to resonate with me as I detailed my view of my role and leadership philosophy. Put simply, I tell my team that my role is to create the conditions for them and their team, as well as for our collective organization, to succeed.

I then follow with my philosophy:

My leadership and management philosophy has three main tenets. These principles will guide my actions:

1. *Know your stuff—be strategically strong and technically sound*

2. *Take care of your team—support the professional and personal success and development of those you lead*

3. *Do the right thing—make decisions that are in the company's best interest*

   My goal is to provide guidance, context, and help you understand why things are important; with that, go about doing your job as you see fit. Unless necessary, I will not tell you how to do your job.
   This philosophy informs both what I expect of you, as well as what you can expect from me.

Clearly documenting and sharing my philosophy and expectations has served me and my teams well in the decades since.

Another great example of developing a clear ethos and writing it down comes from Colin Powell. He had a storied thirty-five-year career as a soldier, rising to the rank of general, and ultimately serving as the chairman of the Joint Chiefs of Staff and later as secretary of state. One piece of writing he is well known for is his "Thirteen Rules," which came to public attention in a *Parade* magazine feature about him in August of 1989. Secretary Powell recalled in his 2012 book *It Worked for Me: In Life and Leadership* how the author of that *Parade* article was looking for a way to close the piece. One of Powell's secretaries suggested the author ask Powell about the couple of dozen snippets of paper shoved under the glass cover on his desk. Powell noted those were, "quotes and aphorisms that I had collected or made up over the years." The author asked Powell to read a few, and the "thirteen I read appeared in a sidebar on the article." Those thirteen snippets scribbled out on scraps of paper, some of which I'm sure were developed after deep thought and introspection, and others likely after a fleeting moment and observation, are some of the most powerful leadership writings I've ever come across (and if you aren't familiar with those Thirteen Rules, I highly encourage you to take five minutes to search for and read them). Scraps of paper turned into a brilliant series of leadership thoughts.

Writing can feel hard. It's not easy to start with a blank slate and develop an output that is something you feel is inspiring and proud of. However, it is worth every minute you devote to it. Committing your thoughts to words, whether on paper or electronically, forces clarity of thought. Making that effort to develop my leadership approach was important in my continued development as a leader. More importantly, taking the time to codify it in words and actually put pen to paper was significant in that it enabled more clear and direct sharing and understanding of that ethos and intent.

In addition to forcing yourself to organize your thoughts and communicate more effectively, setting clear expectations and writing them down can also be a force multiplier. That term is regularly used in the military to describe the factor or factors that can enable personnel or hardware to be more effective and accomplish dramatically greater feats than without it. A force multiplier can make one person or team as effective as ten. One example is a simple radio. Imagine a fire team of four Marines moving individually through the woods as they work toward their objective. The fog of war will inevitably rear its head, and it will be incredibly difficult for those four Marines to coordinate their efforts and achieve their objective. Now imagine each of those Marines with a radio and the ability to communicate and coordinate their efforts. That small group of four now has the ability to be as effective as a group multiple times its size. The radio has become a force multiplier. Setting clear expectations and documenting them can be a force multiplier, as it builds on what might have been individual conversations and expectations and transforms them into coherent and broadly understood guidance for the team.

Take a scrap of paper, and start with a single thought. Add to it the next week, and add another scrap of paper the week after. You are on your way.

If you want to be the best version of yourself, set clear expectations with your team, and commit to documenting them clearly and succinctly.

CHAPTER SEVEN

Focus with a Mantra

If you want to be the best version of yourself,
break down actions into component parts.

MARINES OFTEN TALK ABOUT THE FOG OF
war and how it impacts our planning and execution. At its simplest level, the fog of war is the uncertainty in situational awareness experienced by participants in military operations. This concept was introduced by Prussian military analyst Carl von Clausewitz in 1832 and gained prominence in 1873 when his work was translated into English with the book *On War.*

The fog of war describes the uncertainty one experiences in the information they have, their ability to execute, the capabilities of their enemy, and all the other variables that constantly change during an operation. The fog of war can make the simplest activity excruciatingly difficult and render much prior training ineffective as Marines struggle to take in varying (and often conflicting) pieces of information and make sense of them.

With all the uncertainty in a military operation, a question inevitably arises about how to overcome this fog. There is no cure-all. The fog of war will always exist, no matter how good your intelligence is or what other mitigating steps you take. What you can do, though, is break essential functions down to their essence and work to focus on basic items of training. Don't become paralyzed with inaction, and instead execute core tasks in a repeatable manner.

In basic infantry training, a Marine learns a simple mantra that is repeated over and over: Shoot. Move. Communicate. As a Marine in a firefight, focus on three things. Shoot. Move. Communicate. Do those three things, over and over, and you will be working toward success.

With the seemingly simple *Shoot*, a Marine is also taught this phrase: "I'm up, I shoot and they see me, I'm down." It's shockingly basic but is drilled into our heads as a critical concept of effective fighting.

Next comes *Move* and the important note to never stay in the same place for long. Moving can refer to you as an individual Marine, as well as a larger unit like a four-person fire team or a twelve-person squad.

Finally, *Communicate*. "What do I know? Who needs to know it? Have I told them?" Three simple questions that are all too often overlooked.

Shoot. Move. Communicate. A mantra every Marine learns at the very beginning of their training and continues to exercise throughout their career. This doesn't solve or eliminate the fog of war, but that mantra helps keep Marines focused, remember the basics, and effectively work through the fog of the battlefield.

Mantras aren't just for the infantry, though. naval aviators have their own as well. Soon after arriving in Pensacola, Florida, for naval flight training, every student hears again and again from their instructors: Aviate, Navigate, Communicate.

Aviate. Focus your attention on the most important thing in front of you—when piloting an aircraft, that means focus on flying before anything else. It sounds so simple but is often too easy to forget.

Navigate. Once you have your aircraft under control, then you can start to figure out where you are, where you need to get to, and what corrections you need to make to get there.

Communicate. After ensuring your aircraft is under control and making way toward your intended destination, it's now appropriate to speak with others. Don't get caught in the trap of thinking hard about making a great, Chuck Yeager-sounding radio call before you have complete control of your aircraft. Too often, we spend too much time thinking about what we want to say next and not focusing on what we should be doing.

Aviate, navigate, communicate—know your priorities and tackle those in order. That simple mantra has served thousands of pilots for decades. I can speak from personal experience how those three simple words helped me through challenging nights of flying and helped enable a safe return back to the ship.

There are other mantras that have roots in the military and have permeated into business and popular culture. An oft-cited one is "Slow is smooth, and smooth is fast." This has been a guiding principle for special forces units and is said to have been developed as a training mantra for situations where both speed and precision were critical. It has since transcended its military origins and is often referred to in business, sports, and personal development situations.

After emphasizing the importance of a mantra, let's pause for a moment to better understand exactly what one is. The word "mantra" is derived from two Sanskrit roots: *manas* meaning *mind* or *to think* and *tra* meaning *tool* or *vehicle*. As such, mantras can be considered tools of thought or mind-vehicles; a way to transport us beyond our thoughts and used as a means of harnessing and focusing the mind. A mantra can be almost any phrase or combination of words that help one retain focus and remain present.

The concept of a mantra to guide actions and help navigate the fog of war came back to me as the leader who was building that new sales engineering team back at EnerNOC. With this growing team, I wasn't leading a twenty-plane mission and dealing with the fog of war, but I was building a team that was an integral part of the sales function and dealing with something that could be just as complicated: the fog of business.

Multiple sales reps to work with, each working on multiple opportunities with unique needs. Customer visits. Software demos. Ongoing product training. End-of-quarter deadlines. It was easy for the work to become overwhelming, and as we entered the end of our first year as a team, I could see that we were getting frazzled at times and having trouble focusing on what was most important.

I thought about what success meant for our team and what we wanted to be known for. Concepts that influenced the development of our sales engineering team included these: be entrepreneurs of sales and product; fuse generalized awareness with specialist expertise; and help deals go as fast as they can but not faster. We codified this mindset with our team mantra—Be Right, Be Authoritative, Be Timely. This mantra was developed to instill confidence in our team with not just the demos we gave and deliverables we created but, more importantly, in the manner in which we went about our business.

Be right. First and foremost, sales engineers must provide 100 percent accurate information to every customer, every time.

Be authoritative. Sales engineers will take command of engagements they support and seek resolution in a firm and thoughtful manner. Our team will always speak with one voice.

Be timely. We will respond expeditiously to all requests but not at the expense of numbers one and two.

Not only did the sales engineers live by this mantra, I shared it with the entire sales team so they could always hold us to the high standard we set for ourselves. That mantra became the backbone of everything we did. When one of us was on the verge of succumbing to the fog of business, we were brought back on track by repeating and living it—be right, be authoritative, be timely.

This mantra helped us focus our efforts, hold ourselves to a high standard, and by making that standard public (by sharing it with the sales reps we supported), we enabled others to hold us to that same standard.

A different professional opportunity to take advantage of a mantra came to me in the fall of 2017. I had been at Volta for about a year and had seen our team perform strong work in a very challenging environment. We were growing into new cities and states across the country, developing new roles on the team and filling them out, and facing the pressure of trying to scale an infrastructure business. Not an easy task. You would definitely call what we were going through a subset of the fog of business; I thought of it as the fog of scaling an infrastructure business. With new team members in cities across the country, we needed to be aligned and function on a consistent, repeatable basis.

The mantra for our team that got us through this phase was Execute Effectively, Execute Collaboratively, and Execute with a Smart Sense of Urgency. Each point was then broken down to share what good looked like.

Good project managers execute effectively. They know they need to not just be right in what they do but, more importantly, they ensure every action they take is maximally effective and ensures optimal results for the effort expended. They know failure can be effective if the project was conceived with solid planning, was purposefully executed, and the lessons learned were shared with all.

Good project managers execute collaboratively. They know their project team succeeds only by working together and collaborating. They know it's not possible for one individual to shoulder all the work involved in completing a project. They offer help when they can, accept help when needed, and always share appropriate information.

Good project managers execute with a smart sense of urgency. They are timely in everything they do and maintain a smart sense of urgency and exercise it when appropriate. They exercise good judgment and treat urgent items as they should be treated; similarly, they don't cause undue strain on themselves and the team by misappropriating valuable time when it's not required. Just as important, good project managers know that smooth is fast. They don't move fast just for the sake of moving fast; they know that a well-orchestrated series of actions executed smoothly and professionally is what moves projects forward quickly. Bad project managers rush and end up making avoidable mistakes.

Mantras are often associated with yoga and other forms of meditation. In that context, chanting mantras can help increase your ability to concentrate and focus your attention. Repeating a mantra can be a positive force that eliminates negativity from your mind and calms your emotions. Within the operations team, our mantra was Execute Effectively, Execute Collaboratively, and Execute with a Smart Sense of Urgency.

Outside of yoga and meditation, why is repeating a mantra effective? Our brains are constantly learning and evolving, developing new pathways by the ways the neurons in our brains communicate. Those neural pathways are reinforced and strengthened when a behavior or thought is repeated. Repeating a mantra over and over again employs the mind by giving it something to do, rather than simply trying to ignore the pain or frustration you are experiencing. Put simply, the things we repeat to ourselves matter.

In a business context, especially one where there is uncertainty and an ever-present fog of war, a mantra can have similar benefits. At one level, reciting a mantra can help release stress, and your body will automatically start to relax. Just as importantly, identifying and repeating key components to incorporate into a mantra will reinforce focus and bring discipline to a harried and uncertain work environment.

If you want to be the best version of yourself, find a mantra on which to focus yourself and your efforts.

CHAPTER EIGHT

Little Jobs Aren't Bad Jobs

If you want to be the best version of yourself you can,
run the best damn geedunk you can.

PEOPLE WHO KNOW ME WELL WILL SAY that I'm up for just about anything: New adventures, sports, physical challenges. I'll try just about anything—once—and give it my best shot. Obviously, they have me pegged. What they may not know, though, is the reason behind that.

One of the more enjoyable roles I had in the Marines was as a flight instructor stationed in North Carolina. After new pilots earn their wings, training continues as they start the process of moving on from a training aircraft and begin to specialize in a specific airframe. That was the CH-53E Super Stallion for me, and that training squadron was in Marine Corps Air Station New River in North Carolina.

In the fall of 2001, I had recently finished three years in a fleet squadron based out of Southern California; had completed two overseas deployments; and as a senior captain, had established myself as a strong pilot. My next assignment was to return to that first training squadron a few years after having graduated as a young lieutenant, this time not as a student but as the instructor, helping train the next generation of pilots.

I should note that in every squadron, in addition to flying, pilots are assigned a collateral duty where they lead functional parts of a squadron, like the Maintenance or Operations department. Having been one of the more senior captains in the unit I was leaving, I had earned a coveted role as a future operations officer within the Operations department. Future Ops is responsible for long-range planning, ensuring squadron pilots are prepared for upcoming deployments, and coordinating with other units. It was a sought-after role, and I enjoyed that level of responsibility and authority.

Upon returning to my old unit in New River, though in a new capacity as an instructor and not a student, one of the first stops was to meet with the commanding officer. It was great to meet the CO and learn about his vision for leading the squadron and training new pilots and aircrew. Since he was a busy officer, that conversation was brief. I continued down the hall.

The next stop was to meet the executive officer, or XO. If the CO is equivalent to the CEO of a civilian business, the XO would be the COO. They run the day-to-day operations of the squadron, supervise the different department heads, and the good ones are generally known to be tough SOBs. In fact, one of the best XOs I ever worked with had the callsign Hatchetman, if that gives you a sense of the personality of a good XO.

After some pleasantries with the XO about my trip East and ensuring I had my housing and personal matters taken care of, we started speaking about my flying experience.

"I can see you are an accomplished pilot, Captain Michaels. Night systems instructor, flight leader, aerial refueling instructor, a couple of deployments overseas. Impressive. We can certainly use your experience. You'll be a great addition to the squadron and corps of instructors."

Okay. Off to a good start with the XO.

"We've got some big plans for the coming months. The CO is talking about deploying nearly the entire squadron to Naval Air Station Key West for a few weeks as a training exercise, and that will be a heavy lift for the entire squadron, especially the Operations and Maintenance departments."

I could see where the conversation was going. He needed to assign my collateral duty and was setting the stage for what was surely a plum assignment by referencing the Ops and the Maintenance departments.

There is a pecking order when it comes to these assignments. Working in the Maintenance and Operations departments is considered the most converted. Maintenance officers get to spend time with Marines on the flight line and lead larger groups. Operations work entails developing training plans for the squadron and ultimately deciding who flies on what missions. Those are the places you want to be.

There are other roles, like leading the Logistics function, and even further down the line is being an administrative officer. Perhaps the lowest rung on the ladder? The S-5 officer. It's hard to succinctly say exactly what the S-5 officer is responsible for; it doesn't even have a catchy name, just an odd-sounding alpha-numeric combination.

"So, Captain Michaels, you are going to be our S-5 officer. There is another officer rotating out of that duty, and he's leaving for a new unit in a few days, so be sure to debrief with him ASAP. Otherwise, it's good to have you aboard. Carry on."

What just happened?

The easiest way to put it is that the S-5 officer is responsible for all the stuff no one else wants to do. That's why they give it to the new guy. Me.

One of the more visible functions of the S-5 is running the gee-dunk. Geedunk is a World War II-era term used to refer to a small snack bar. It's often a tiny, nondescript room where a Marine can take a short break and quickly grab a soda or candy bar before getting back to work fixing helicopters on the flight line.

When you run the geedunk, you get to go into town and buy cases of drinks and boxes of snacks from the local warehouse store, then oversee selling them in that small room near the squadron flightline so they can be available to Marines who are looking for a quick snack and a cool drink. This is the exact opposite of what senior captains want to do. Managing the selling of sodas and chips is neither adventurous nor cool, nor the kind of thing you want to write home about.

As I continued checking in and making the rounds of the squadron, one of my final stops of the day was Flight Equipment, the department that manages flight vests, helmets, and other aviation safety equipment. The staff sergeant in charge greeted me and inquired about where I'd be working when I wasn't flying. I answered that my collateral duty was the S-5. I suspect he could see a lack of bounce in my step.

"Can I tell you something, Captain? I'm coming up on twenty years as a Marine. It's inevitable that we all will eventually get an assignment we didn't ask for. If there is anything I've learned, it's that if you are going to do anything, then do it right. Run the best damn geedunk you can. The Marines will appreciate it." And there it was. "Run the best damn geedunk you can."

Soon after, my responsibilities increased, though not necessarily in the way I desired. The S-5 is responsible for more than just the geedunk. I found that out in a subsequent conversation with the XO.

"Captain Michaels. Congratulations. You are in charge of the squadron birthday ball this year. The general will be there. Make sure it's great. Don't screw it up."

"Yes, Sir." *Not much more to say than that.*

Once again, we are not talking about the glamorous role of leading Marines down on the flight line or determining flight schedules and who is going to get coveted night vision goggle flight hours.

Marines take the birthday of the Corps very seriously. On November 10 every year, we say "Happy Birthday" to one another as if it was our own birthday. We sing about the birthday while running in formation ... "Back in 1775, my Marine Corps came alive!" is a popular ditty. The birthday ball is a significant event. Planning for it entails picking a menu, organizing music and decorations, coordinating a guest of honor, and being responsible for the ceremonial aspect of the celebration; it's not unlike planning a wedding. It needs to be done, and the new guy on the block gets to do it.

Marines often use the colloquial phrase "Embrace the suck" when talking about how to make the best of any (usually bad) situation. You need to deal with it and take it in stride. Embrace the suck.

Throughout the rest of my career, both in the Marines and as a civilian, I was asked to run a lot of geedunks. There was mail to open, plants to water, floors to clean, and there were times when *I* needed to do those tasks. With every menial task, every job that I felt was below my title or job level, I looked back on my time running the S-5, buying candy bars and sodas for the geedunk and choosing music for the birthday ball. Much like Admiral McRaven observes in *The Wisdom of the Bullfrog*, I've found that if you take pride in your work and the results achieved in doing those little jobs, people would think you are worthy of bigger jobs.

We all run a geedunk at some point, so if you want to be the best version of yourself you can, run the best damn geedunk you can.

CHAPTER NINE

Getting the Question Right
Is More Important
than Having the Answer

If you want to be the best version of yourself that you can,
shift from having answers to asking questions.

RUNNING WAS NOT ALWAYS A PASSION OF mine. Soccer was a big part of my life as a kid, and being a midfielder meant that I needed great endurance, but running cross country or even just a casual couple-mile jog was not something I regularly did growing up.

Running became more of an activity for me as I prepared to go to OCS; it was hard to know exactly what to predict about what would happen once there, but one common theme among everyone I spoke to was that as an officer candidate, you had better show up in excellent physical condition.

I ran throughout my years in the Marines for a few reasons. One was simply to stay in good physical condition. The other was to ensure I was prepared for the twice-yearly physical fitness test.

There are no more PFTs once you leave the Marines, though, and no more timed three-mile runs. Somewhere during my years of service, though, I became what I call "a runner." For me, that was enjoying the peace of a morning jog, with nothing but my thoughts for company. No headphones. No earbuds. Just the thump-thump of shoes on the pavement and rhythmic breathing that for me is somewhat meditative. That continued as I moved back to California, though as a civilian this time, and got into trail running along the Pacific coast.

Just because I enjoy the relaxing aspect of running doesn't mean I left behind all my competitive spirit upon leaving the Marines. When the clock is ticking, I'm always looking to perform at my best. I soon discovered trail half-marathons in the Bay Area and had some small degree of success in those runs, usually finishing in the top ten for my age group. That was satisfying for me, until the morning of the 2014 Big Sur Half Marathon.

Our family ventured down the coast toward Monterey for this race, and I was in prime condition. I was limbering up as the course marshal gave instructions over a bullhorn. There was excitement in the air, with hundreds of runners gathered for multiple races. It was one of those mornings where everything just feels right and you know it's going to be a good day; your legs and lungs are primed, and you feel a good time coming. The two longest runs that day were the marathon and half-marathon. We all were to start together and run toward a turnaround point; the marathoners would keep going, while the half-marathoners would turn around and head back to the finish. The marshal was rambling on about the different landmarks and points on the course . . . some kind of details that I wasn't listening to. I was in the zone and ready for a great run.

The starting gun sounded, and we took off. The first few strides confirmed my feeling this was going to be a strong race. Every stride felt smooth in the cool Pacific morning.

I tend to start toward the back of most races. Some runners aim to start at the front and get out early. Starting further back helps me to not go out too fast, and, more importantly, becomes a little game I play, picking off runners one by one as I work my way toward the front of the pack. *I'm going to pass him. She's next. Him . . . I'm going to pass him in the next minute.*

That morning was no different as I steadily climbed the mountain and moved my way through the pack. The marshal had said something back at the pre-race briefing about the halfway point and when the marathon would diverge from the half-marathon.

Not recalling the exact instructions he gave, I remember thinking, *I'll find that point easily; just keep running and don't stop.* At this point it was fun to pass the other runners. I remember one in a bright orange top. Another with a purple hat.

Coming around a bend, there was a runner ahead coming back toward me. That must have been the first runner in the half-marathon to hit the turnaround point and start back down the mountain. A few moments later, another runner was bounding down. *Perfect; now I can know exactly where I am in the pack. I just need to count the runners who have turned around and are coming back down.*

Four. Five. Seven. Seven. Seven. *Could I be in eighth place overall? Not a top ten in my age division, but a top ten overall?*

No one else was coming back down, and up ahead was an aid station. *I could use some water before the final push to the top and the turnaround point.*

Some runners stop at aid stations to grab a quick snack and eat. My style is to spend as little time as possible there. Get a quick drink and pick up valuable seconds in moving toward the number-one position.

This aid station was busy, with all the different races sharing the same course that morning. Having downed a quick drink, I looked at the nearest support staff I could find and asked, "Which way?"

With a moment's pause, just a half a second, she pointed ahead and declared, "That way!"

That was all the info I needed as I sprinted off downhill and my stride lengthened and pace quickened. I could only imagine how I'd feel upon hitting the halfway point and blasting through the second half of the course. The crowd of runners thinned out, and a few minutes later I began to wonder where the halfway point was. *It must be here soon. I haven't seen the eighth runner coming back, so I still must be in eighth place.*

There it was around the next bend. An aid station. The halfway point! Cruising in and picking up a cup of water I asked in a confident voice, "This is the halfway point, right?"

"For what, the marathon? No, you still have a way to go," came the reply.

"Wait. What?" *Don't tell me I've done what I think I've done.*

"Yeah, the turnaround point on the half marathon is back up the hill. The way you came from."

Shit.

There's a moment when you know you've made a mistake, and it's hard to swallow. I had run past the half marathon turnaround point and to the next aid station on the marathon course. It was time to about-face and head back up that hill to the larger aid station and turnaround point I should have noticed all those precious minutes ago.

I made it back to that aid station, skipped the drink, and started back down. *No top-ten finish for me today,* I thought as I picked off runners on the way back down. The one with the orange shirt. The purple hat. Passed them for the second time that morning. They seemed to be enjoying themselves and having a fun morning. Not me.

I don't remember what place I finished at that morning; I really didn't want to know. My wife will tell you that I still talk about that day and get frustrated every time I do. *What happened? How did I miss something so obvious like a significant turnaround point on a race?*

Some component of my brain was not listening to the instructions the marshal gave at the pre-race briefing; I suspect he clearly detailed them. Even without listening, though, I could have turned around at the right point and worked my way into the top five. Instead, I asked a poorly worded question, "Which way?" Of course someone on the half-marathon would have known to turn around, so the obvious situation was that the runner asking was on the marathon, and the clear answer was to point to the marathon course and shout, "That way!"

I asked the wrong question and received an answer that might have been factually correct but was very much not the answer I was looking for.

A few years later I was faced with a challenging professional dilemma. I had recently taken over as the head of Operations at Volta at a time when growth was paramount. We were racing to increase the pace at which we installed electric vehicle charging stations. While construction is never easy and is often fraught with setbacks and delays, we faced a bigger challenge with the final commissioning process before marking a project as complete. An electric vehicle charging station is a combination of many different technologies—both hardware and software—and getting all the different systems to integrate and work as a whole often took longer to troubleshoot than the actual process of digging holes in the ground and performing the installation. The proper firmware needed to be installed on various components (that might have been shipped from different manufacturers months prior), and cellular connectivity was always a challenge (especially if the charging station was in a parking garage).

Our construction project managers had tough jobs. The bulk of their work commenced after permits were secured, and they were primarily focused on managing the contractors who would perform the actual installations. Getting all the hardware successfully installed was an accomplishment, and troubleshooting the dozens of little things required to finalize the project became a major point of frustration. Little steps were easy to miss, and it was hard to remember to complete and check all the little things that needed to be done. After a project was marked as complete, it was somewhat common for that station to become a maintenance issue the next day as we had missed some seemingly insignificant but important step at the end of the project. As the project had been officially deemed complete, the construction project manager was no longer involved, and our Service team inherited an issue to fix that never should have been a complete project in the first place.

I could see where this was going. Getting to the root cause was going to expose gaps in our workflows and likely mean some additional work for the construction project managers. That would not be popular. Having been a Marine and pilot for nearly ten years, I was a firm believer in the power of checklists; even though a pilot might know by heart the steps to start up an aircraft, they would never dream of initiating that process without the checklist in hand and one pilot reading steps while the other performed them and made verbal confirmation. Though that additional work needed to be done, I felt there was a better way than simply barking an order to "work harder and don't forget important steps." That's hard news to hear from the new guy. *How could I get the message across to our team about not trying to remember all the steps that needed to be completed in order to successfully complete a project?*

I wasn't going to tell the team what to do . . . they were going to figure it out for themselves by reading, discovering, and coming to a conclusion without me telling them anything.

I had read *Checklist Manifesto* by Atul Gawande years earlier and knew the book was perfect for this situation. He was a surgeon who had been trying to understand the source of difficulties and stresses in the practice of medicine. Medical care had become more and more complex, and that complexity was putting enormous strain to doctors and making it harder for them—and their patients—to realize the benefits of the advancements that were being made. The complexity of practicing medicine had exceeded a doctor's ability to deliver its benefits correctly, safely, and reliably. Additional knowledge had helped doctors greatly and at the same time had burdened them greatly.

The book goes beyond just examples of how checklists had profound significance in hospitals and also covers examples from aviation, disaster response, and construction.

Ah, I'm not going to tell them about the importance of checklists; it will be better if they come to that conclusion on their own.

I assigned the book for reading as part of an upcoming team offsite. At that meeting, we spent a few hours discussing the book and what the team thought about it. I asked some questions that ranged from, "What did you think about the part . . . " to "Were checklists worth the added time and effort?" and "Why do you think we read this book together?"

The discussion started by focusing on hospitals and other scenarios the author had investigated and soon turned to operations work.

One member of team somewhat hesitantly commented, "You know, we could set up some checklists, and it wouldn't be too hard."

That was followed by a slightly more positive, "Yeah, we could have a checklist that the project manager uses and have another member of the team confirm the items are complete and get a second set of eyes on the work before we mark the project complete."

We spent another hour getting into the details and walked away from that offsite with our first ever charging station commissioning checklist. It covered all the seemingly insignificant but actually important steps that needed to be completed before marking a project as complete. The team came to that realization with just a few prompting questions from me.

The best part of the offsite, though, was a comment that came a few days later.

"Do you have another book for us, Jon?"

That's when that first reading turned into the Operations Book Club, where once or twice a year the entire team would read a different book. The topics varied from how to improve operational efficiency to personal and professional development ideas. The common theme, though, was that we read a book that spoke to a specific challenge or stage of growth we were facing at that time. Rather than hear me drone on about a particular topic, we all read the same book at the same time and came away with a common understanding. I suspect you can still ask any of those members about what is *The Goal,* the difference between complex and complicated, what Legos have to do with systems growth, or what it means to be "the Herbie," and they will tell you.

My takeaway was that asking the right question—"What is the challenge we are facing as a team, and what is the best way to help develop a communal knowledge and understanding to work toward overcoming it?"—was more important than coming to the table with a perceived right answer in hand.

Albert Einstein, arguably one of the greatest minds of modern times, is reported to have said, "If I had an hour to solve a problem and my life depended on the solution, I would spend the first fifty-five minutes determining the proper question to ask . . . for once I know the proper question, I could solve the problem in less than five minutes."

As genius as Einstein was, I believe there are yet additional variables to consider when it comes to asking questions. First, we should explore the concept of systems thinking. Systems thinking is an approach to problem-solving that views problems as part of a broader, dynamic system. It is the process of understanding how things influence one another as part of a whole. We can't simply consider one variable in isolation; rather, we need to take a step back and consider the wider ecosystem.

Then there is the concept of cognitive bias or preferences. These biases are caused by the tendency of the human brain to simplify information by processing it through a filter of personal experience and preferences. A simple explanation is that since I am a veteran of the Marines, I have a natural tendency to gravitate toward, and perhaps give preference to, other veterans and Marines. We tend to like individuals and give preference to those who are like us. We tend to get news from the same sources that we are comfortable with. We tend to read the same kind of books, and that can lead to more recommendations that we read even more of the same types of material. Problem is, we usually don't recognize the presence of those biases.

So, how do we get past these cognitive biases? Explore the concepts of cognitive diversity and creative abrasion. Cognitive diversity encompasses the variety of ways in which different people think. We all process information, see the world, and make decisions in different ways. That cognitive diversity is amplified if we can embrace it in a productive way. If we can then get that diversity into a room (real or virtual) together and constructively combine those different approaches, experiences, and values, we have the concept of creative abrasion; the intellectual friction that hones ideas into their most-perfect versions through vigorous debate of diverse perspectives.

Back to systems thinking and our Operations Book Club. If I could do it again, it wouldn't be just me trying to identify the challenges the team was facing and being susceptible to my echo-chamber of reading history. Rather, there would be a team approach to identify the big issues we needed to address and input from different perspectives on the questions to ask and the joint reading material to get us there.

If you want to be the best version of yourself that you can, systematically ask the right questions at the right time and in the right way.

CHAPTER TEN

Never Stop Learning

*If you want to be the best version of yourself,
have a beginner's mindset.*

IF YOU WERE TO ASK MY WIFE, COVAHNE, about this book, she would likely tell you it should have a different title. She would call it *You Said Yes to What? Lessons From Living With Someone Who Has Lost His Mind.* There might very well be a good reason for that.

It was a typical weekday evening as I sat on our living room couch, scrolling through websites, searching for a trail run to sign up for. Though I had left active duty a decade earlier, the Marine mindset of always having a challenge to work toward had stayed with me. I was on the hunt for my next one. By luck, or fate, an ad popped up on my laptop advertising the Escape from Alcatraz Duathlon.

Alcatraz. It holds a place of mystery in the minds of Americans, especially those who live in San Francisco. It's impossible not to have your eyes drawn to it every time one heads down to the water. Surrounded by cold water, sometimes impenetrable fog, and the idea (real or not) of ever-present sharks helps Alcatraz hold a unique place in our minds.

Jump off a ferry stationed next to the island, swim nearly one-and-a-half miles into Aquatic Park and then run a seven-miles to the base of the Golden Gate Bridge and back? *Perfect!* I had my next challenge lined up.

Eager to share this fantastic idea with Covahne, I caught her as she walked down the hallway. "Guess what I just signed up for? This is going to be great!"

"Are. You. Crazy?" was her initial response. She had always been supportive of my goals and activities. This endeavor was off to a rocky start.

"C'mon, everyone who lives in San Francisco does the Alcatraz swim at some point."

"No. They don't," was her swift reply. "We've lived here for years and don't know anyone who has done that. Besides, have you ever swum in a race before?"

"No."

"Have you ever swum in the ocean before?"

Well, there was that annual trip to the beach when I was a kid to jump up and down in the waves.

"No."

Her next question hung in the air. "And you think this is a good way to start?"

The uneasy silence passed after some awkward minutes.

A few days later I was off to the local sports equipment store to learn about the gear I would want for this adventure. I was introduced to a different world of goggles, wetsuits (yes, wetsuit or not is a divisive topic in San Francisco, but that's another topic), and other gear needed to start ocean swimming. That, and a few tips from the very helpful salesperson, and I was on my way.

The first few trips to Aquatic Park were hard. It's a popular spot along San Francisco Bay and filled with both serious and recreational swimmers. The views are breathtaking, the water cold. I quickly learned I was on the recreational end of the spectrum after a few minutes in the water. I knew how to swim, as we'd had to demonstrate that during flight school. This was much harder. The first thirty minutes in the unforgiving ocean highlighted that while I was physically able to swim, coaching would significantly improve my form and overall performance in the water.

My next stop was my good friend Crosby, a varsity water polo player from Stanford who was more than comfortable in the water. He evaluated my stroke and provided some much-needed advice. He could have dissuaded me from participating in the race, but instead his feedback started with, "I can see you know how to swim and am pretty sure you will survive the race."

Thanks, Crosby. Covahne will be happy to hear your vote of confidence.

He continued, "I could give you twenty things to work on, but here's three to focus on as you continue training. Small improvements to your technique will make a huge difference." Crosby provided some advice on my head position, body position, and how to move my arms when they were out of the water; things that seem so simple but actually require coaching and practice to execute properly and benefit from.

My next step was to actively solicit advice from triathletes and others experienced in not just swimming but transitioning from one component of a race to another.

Meanwhile, I'd been putting in the weekly miles and kept up with the running. This is where the regaining and embracing my beginner's mindset really started to pay off. I spent that first month thinking a lot about body position while swimming; hey, that's important in running, too. Same with breathing. Same with something even as simple as prepping to head out for a run/swim and how to put myself in the position to have a great workout. Suddenly, I found myself re-energized about running after working to improve my swimming. I did more than just learn to swim; I turned into a better runner, too.

The morning of the race came. It was a classic, foggy day in the Bay. The swimmers boarded the ferry and headed out to the dock at Alcatraz. When the all-clear sign came, a horn was blown, and the race was underway.

The cold water was a shock when I jumped off the ferry and into the Bay. I was disoriented by the hundreds of other swimmers in close proximity as we all started our way to Aquatic Bay. It took me a long time to get my breathing under control and get comfortable in the water, significantly longer than in any of my practice swims. So long, in fact, that as my wife and boys waited on shore for me, they had to wait much longer than expected until I finally made my way out of the water. *I'm alive, and I made it! Oh yea, now I have to go complete the run . . .*

I didn't realize it at the time, but my approach to learning how to swim in the ocean was a methodical one. I started with setting a very clear goal and declared it publicly (to my wife and friends), who helped keep me accountable. I embraced a growth mindset; the belief that one can develop the necessary skills and by putting in the effort to learn, one can actually build those skills. The next step was to embrace active learning—the best way to become an ocean swimmer is to actually swim in the ocean. I paired active learning with embracing different learning approaches. I watched videos, read articles, and sought out experts to learn from. Finally, I made use of deliberate practice that involved intentional, goal-directed rehearsal. I would spend one training session focused on my head position, and the next day I would focus on my body position. After deliberately practicing those individual components, I worked to put them together and execute them all at once. I'm convinced it was because I embraced a beginner's mindset and one of continuous learning that I was able to complete that swim.

This mindset has helped me in more than just swimming; it's helped me become a better leader. I've found that regaining and embracing a beginner's mindset and translating that energy, enthusiasm, and desire to learn back into areas I have already experienced, such as leadership, has helped me improve and build upon skills I thought were my already strong skills.

Learning about the fundamentals of swimming inspired me to think about how I prepare for, run, and follow-up after leading a meeting. I have sometimes fallen prey to the ease of winging it and not leading as effective meetings as I could. Taking time to revisit simple concepts around leading meetings has paid huge dividends for my teams and me.

Similarly, I've invested time to read and consult with others about how I provide feedback and have effective one-on-ones with my team. I thought about that a lot years ago as a first-time manager, and my takeaways from swimming encouraged me to pursue some refresher training that helped both my employees and me.

As children, we learn nonstop about our surroundings and are constantly exploring the world around us. Then comes school and more formal method instruction in academic subjects such as math and science, though we continue to learn in less formal ways, such as through social interactions and hobbies. Learning continues after college, as we get our first jobs and learn about the specific responsibilities therein as well as intangibles such as office politics.

There is a trap that is easy to fall into after we've achieved some level of experience and expertise in our current job. Learning moves from being something considered mandatory or expected and instead can start to feel optional. We might not feel the need to learn and can get by with an occasional minor update of a skill or function.

Then comes a choice: Do we continue learning or simply stop because we want more time to relax or believe we've learned enough to date and have graduated from that requirement? Choosing the latter leads to a cycle of complacency and atrophy of this crucial skill.

I am sometimes a glutton for punishment and signed up the next year for another swim under the Golden Gate Bridge, starting by jumping from a ferry by the south tower and swimming across the main channel to Point Cavallo on the north side of the Bay. I maintained my beginner's mindset, continued to learn and practice, and completed what was perhaps the hardest physical challenge I've ever had.

Take a risk. It's the best way to push yourself, learn, and maintain that beginner's mindset.

If you want to be the best version of yourself, have a beginner's mindset, and be a lifelong learner.

CLOSING

SO, WHAT TO DO WITH THESE SEEMINGLY disparate ideas, stories, and lessons? While I trust (notice I didn't say hope) they each have proven helpful in some way, what happens after you turn the last page and put the book down? Go on with your life and see if you can remember something here for more than two minutes? Something else? There must be more, right?

I challenge you to not focus too much on my personal events and the stories I have told here. Take them for what they are: Stories from my past that, upon some reflection, have had great meaning for me. Yes, there are many universal lessons and takeaways from those events, and perhaps you will benefit from them in some small way.

Rather, a better outcome would be to identify your own foundational events and stories. Those events have happened to you, and you just may need to commit the time to reflecting and identifying them. How do you identify these?

It's never in the moment and likely not in the ensuing weeks— you are too busy processing what just happened to be able to consider a longer-term perspective. I've found in some instances that in the ensuing months, I realized something interesting had happened, though that's not sufficient to truly glean a meaningful personal or professional lesson. For me it's often been a few years before I was able to look back with some sense of clarity and recognition on what happened on the day in question and the significance it would hold.

This means there is ample opportunity for all of you to look back on those days when you recognized that something interesting had happened and reflect on how that day has impacted your way of thinking, acting, and leading. I've found that it's the days and events I have told stories about that are the ones that have been consequential to me. The stories you tell your friends over a drink. The stories you tell colleagues and employees at work. The stories you tell your spouse or significant other and family around the dinner table. If you are telling a story that many times to that many people, odds are it represents a big part of who you are and is one that has shaped you personally and professionally, likely without you even realizing it.

Just as important, after identifying those key events and associated lessons learned, you need to have the discipline to implement them into your daily operating rhythm. That operating rhythm is the combination of the things you do, the way you do them, and the cadence of how you go about your day.

Having a cadence like that takes discipline, and that self-discipline is the most important personal and professional quality a person can have. Discipline is what takes well-intentioned thoughts and turns them into thoughtful action.

I've often been asked what I think is an important leadership characteristic. By far, I see that is self-discipline. Imagine we take ten leaders chosen at random and ask them to write what they believe are the most important qualities in a leader. Regardless of how competent those leaders are, I suspect the ten lists they generate would have a lot of overlap and similarities. As an example, I bet many of those lists would contain something to the effect of "Spend time with your team so you can have a deep understanding of their role and their day" and "Communicate a clear and meaningful mission and vision." Easy to say, but how many of those ten randomly chosen leaders actually do spend time with their team in order to have a deep understanding of what they do? How many leaders actually spend the time to develop and communicate a clear mission and vision? Not all ten. So, while it's easy to espouse whatever it is that you think are important leadership qualities, it is self-discipline that leads you to actually execute those on a regular basis.

Discipline. What exactly is that, and how does it manifest itself? The answer will vary for each individual. I can't tell you what to be disciplined about . . . only you can figure that out for yourself. What I can offer, though, is the belief that exercising discipline is crucial to your development as a person.

I started doing one hundred pushups every day back in February of 2022 and have been doing that every day since. Why do I keep doing this? When I hit the one-year mark I asked myself if I would keep going and maintain the streak. *For the sake of the streak?* That kept me going for a while. It can be a grind doing one hundred pushups every day, and while I continued to do them I continued to ask myself, *Why?* Somewhere around day six hundred, I realized that those one hundred pushups were my way of maintaining *my discipline*. The discipline of doing one hundred pushups every day is symbolic to me in demonstrating the discipline I strive for in other aspects of my life. It works for me.

Find the things that work for you, and have the discipline to actually do them and not just talk about it.

It can be yoga, meditation, reading, volunteering . . . or any of a hundred other things. What's important is that you find that thing for yourself and be disciplined about it. Not simply for the sake of saying you do something every day; that's the wrong reason. The reason is to develop that internal self-discipline that is crucial to developing as a leader and more importantly as a spouse, partner, parent, friend, and individual.

So remember: Focus on the little things, take the invisible path when you can, and don't be afraid to admit when you've screwed up. Set a North Star and establish clear expectations of yourself and others, and find a mantra to help you focus along the way. Own your choices, and work on asking strong questions. Embrace a beginner's mindset, as it will help you run the geedunk you will inevitably be asked to lead. And always look to say yes when a meaningful opportunity comes your way. If you do these things, and look to find your own foundational lessons to learn from, you'll be on your way to being the best version of yourself.